THE
AESTHETICS
OF
COMICS

ALSO BY DAVID CARRIER

with Mark Roskill, *Truth and Falsity in Visual Images*
Artwriting
Principles of Art History Writing
Poussin's Paintings: A Study in Art-Historical Methodology
*The Aesthete in the City: The Philosophy and Practice of American Abstract
    Painting in the 1980s*
Nicolas Poussin: Lettere sull'arte
High Art: Charles Baudelaire and the Origins of Modernism
England and Its Aesthetes: Biography and Taste
Garner Tullis: The Life of Collaboration

THE AESTHETICS OF COMICS

DAVID CARRIER

THE PENNSYLVANIA STATE UNIVERSITY PRESS
UNIVERSITY PARK, PENNSYLVANIA © 2000

Library of Congress Cataloging-in-Publication Data

Carrier, David, 1944–
The aesthetics of comics / David Carrier.
p.   cm.
Includes bibliographical references and index.
ISBN 0-271-01962-X (cl. : alk. paper)
1. Comic books, strips, etc.—History and criticism.   I. Title.
PN6710.C35   2000
741.5′01—DC21   99-17980
CIP

This book is for my nana, Mary Farcher (1897–1993);
for my parents, Walter Carrier (1918–1999) and Louise F. Carrier;
for my wife, Marianne L. Novy;
and for my daughter, Liz.

CONTENTS

LIST OF ILLUSTRATIONS

On the dedication page: the author at the age of eight, reading comics.

ACKNOWLEDGMENTS

I was first inspired to write this book when my daughter, Liz, was young and I read Tintin to her at bedtime. Seeing how much she liked comics, and recalling my own youthful pleasure in them, I wanted to explain why they are so fascinating. Liz now is too old to be read to at bedtime, but I hope she will read this book when she grows up. After I finished the manuscript, my parents unearthed a photograph of me as a child reading a comic book. The dedication is a thank-you to four generations of my family. My father knew that he was one of the family members to whom this book was dedicated. How much I regret that he did not live to receive it.

I also thank Kermit S. Champa, Aneta Georgievska-Shine, Michele Hannoosh, Richard Kuhns, Marianne L. Novy, and Richard Shiff for comments on earlier drafts, and Paul Barolsky, who successfully persuaded me that the best books are short books. Christopher Couch shared with me his comics bibliography, John Elderfield discussed his work in progress on Matisse, Sir Ernst Gombrich spoke of his passion for this art form, Thomas Nozkowski provided some great examples, and Gary Schwartz introduced me to the art of Charlotte Salomon. My ideas about how to describe visual art owe much to Catherine Lee, Sylvia Plimick Mangold and Robert Mangold, Robert Ryman, and Garner Tullis. Like everything I have written in the past seventeen years, this book has been decisively influenced by Sean Scully.

I published a much earlier version of a small portion of Chapter 1 as "He Dreams She Dreams of Him," in *Puzzles About Art: An Aesthetics Casebook,* ed. M. Battin, J. Fisher, R. Moore, and A. Silvers (New York: St. Martins Press, 1989). Related materials appear as chapter 4 of my *High Art: Charles Baudelaire and the Origins of Modernism* (University Park: Pennsylvania State University Press, 1996). Portions of this book were presented in very different forms as "Andy Warhol's Moving Pictures of

Modern Life," *Source* 16, no. 3 (1997): 30–34; "The Pleasures of Stupidity: Gary Larson as a Baudelairian Caricaturist," *Nineteenth-Century French Studies* 27, nos. 1–2 (1998–99): 62–70; and "Piero della Francesca, Hergé, and George Herriman: Comics and the Art of Moving Pictures," *Word & Image* 13, no. 4 (1997): 317–32. I have given lectures using this material at the University of Western Ontario, London, Canada, thanks to Mark Cheetham; the New York Studio School and a 1996 session of the College Art Association organized by Nan Rosenthal and Richard Shiff, where Ann Gibson provided commentary; the Department of Art and Design, Division of Arts and Humanities, Grand Valley State University; the University of Auckland and the Victoria University of Wellington, New Zealand; the Andy Warhol Museum, Pittsburgh; and the Twenty-Ninth International Conference on the History of Art, Amsterdam, 1996; the philosophy department, University of Richmond; and the art history department, Swarthmore College. Many artists gave me comics I otherwise would never have discovered. I wish to thank Keith Monley for patiently reliable editing, and Sandy Thatcher, director of Penn State Press, for taking much time to help me to understand the copyright laws relating to comics. Interlibrary-loan librarians at my university offered essential assistance. I thank also the patient chairman of my department, Wilfried Sieg.

Academic books like mine are difficult and expensive to produce. Regretting that the refusal of the copyright owners to provide material at affordable prices has deprived this volume of any illustration of the art of Gary Larson and Hergé and has made it impossible to include a reproduction of the Daumier painting discussed by Roger Fry in the account presented in Chapter 5, I am thankful to the many publishers who responded generously to my queries.

Bill Berkson and Arthur C. Danto read this book for Penn State Press, making many suggestions I have used. Philip Winsor, my editor, provided consistently helpful advice. After the manuscript was completed, I spent a semester at Princeton University, where, in an interview with me, Alexander Nehamas spoke of "the importance of appearance in general, that most, so to speak, *overlooked* aspect of things among philosophers, with their emphasis on clunky, boring, deadly depth." He gave me reason to think that a philosophical study of comics was worthwhile. Our discussions about television and perspectivism, and the importance of clear writing, significantly influenced my final revision of this text.

How lucky I am to have so many generous supporters.

THE REALM OF SPIRIT IS DARK AND DIFFICULT *TERRA INCOGNITA* SO FAR
AS PHILOSOPHICAL UNDERSTANDING IS CONCERNED, THOUGH IT IS AS
WELL, SO FAR AS HUMAN UNDERSTANDING IS CONCERNED, THE MOST
FAMILIAR TERRITORY OF ALL. IT IS IN THE REALM OF SPIRIT THAT WE
EXIST AS HUMAN BEINGS.

—ARTHUR C. DANTO, *CONNECTIONS TO THE WORLD*

This book is the first by an analytic philosopher to identify and solve the
aesthetic problems posed by comic strips and to explain the relationship
of this artistic genre to other forms of visual art. I distinguish comics from
traditional static images—paintings, engravings, and other prints—and
from movies, pictures that when projected move automatically. That I
sometimes use disagreements about points of detail to motivate the presentation should not obscure my enormous debt to the great pioneering
discussions: Ernst Gombrich's essays on caricature; David Kunzle's two-
volume history of the comic strip; the 1991 exhibition catalogue *High and
Low* by Kirk Varnedoe and Adam Gopnik; and Scott McCloud's *Understanding Comics: The Invisible Art*. Alexander Nehamas's essays on television gave me the idea that a popular art form deserves serious
philosophical attention. My conception of a posthistorical art derives
from Arthur C. Danto's writings. Michele Hannoosh's book on caricature
showed me how to relate present-day comics to the discussion of aesthetic
theory in my own book on Baudelaire. A fully illustrated history of the
comic strip would be a large, fat, expensive volume. Because my focus in

this slim book is on conceptual issues, I refer the reader to the readily accessible commercial volumes that provide a rich survey of examples.

Comic strips, intrinsically fascinating, raise as-yet-little-discussed problems of great interest; analysis of comics suggests novel ways of understanding the history of visual art. Philosophers dealing with visual art very naturally focus their attention on theory-bound works—on old-master art that has subtle iconography and on modernist artifacts that exist as art only in relation to discourse about theory. Comics, by contrast, are like pop music—an art form almost all of us understand without any need for theorizing. The great discovery of high art was that it was possible to narrate highly complex scenes without any appeal to words. The equally surprising discovery of the comics was that it is possible to deploy many different kinds of verbal information within storytelling visual images. Although this book focuses on comics, the argument is of broader relevance. McCloud's positively Gombrichian willingness to appeal to experimental evidence should be suggestive to historians of art and philosophers interested in the nature of perception.

Aestheticians and art historians have justifiably devoted a great deal of attention to visual representation. Until we understand the different ways in which Giotto and Raphael depict textures, Ruisdael and Constable show clouds, and Poussin and Caravaggio express emotion, we are hardly able to understand how we respond to their pictures. With comics, similarly, until we properly grasp how their particular combination of words and pictures functions, how can we evaluate them critically (and politically) or understand their relation to high art? My goal is Gombrich's—"finding out what role the image may play in the household of our mind."[1] Film studies have become an important academic concern. It is very odd that, by contrast, the comics have attracted so little academic attention, for they have a much larger audience and raise problems as interesting as paintings'.[2]

Comics have not been properly understood by aestheticians, because as yet the essential philosophical issues they deal with have not been identified. Everyone acknowledges that Poussin's paintings deserve philosophi-

---

1. E. H. Gombrich, *Meditations on a Hobby Horse* (London: Phaidon, 1963), 127.
2. It is a great misfortune that the reissue of the most famous early comic, *Krazy Kat*, never was realized. "Surely the prerequisite for serious evaluation of any artist's or writer's contributions is that the work under consideration be accessible" (Rosemont, "Surrealism in the Comics I: Krazy Kat [George Herriman]," in *Popular Culture in America*, ed. Paul Buhle [Minneapolis: University of Minnesota, 1987], 123). What major painter lacks a *catalogue raisonné*?

cally informed commentary. But slight popular images, art that everyone understands without need of any explanation, could they also deserve the attention of philosophers? Modern philosophy owes much to the close study of humble examples—to Jean-Paul Sartre's and Maurice Merleau-Ponty's phenomenological studies of desire, John Austin's account of ordinary language, Ludwig Wittgenstein's analysis of games, and G. E. M. Anscombe's account of intention. What remains unachieved is a proper understanding of the implications of these concerns for aesthetics. Much of this book was written with Arthur C. Danto's *Connections to the World: The Basic Concepts of Philosophy* on one side of my powerbook and the various histories of comics on the other.[3] Adapting the exemplary structure of Danto's *Jean-Paul Sartre*, each chapter here has two titles, one relating to comics, the other alluding to related issues from within philosophy. My dual concerns, art-historical and philosophical, thus run through the entire book. Appeal to these philosophical concerns is not a merely literary embellishment of my commentary. To understand comics properly, I am arguing, we must identify the conceptual issues posed by their definition and interpretation.

What is a comic? The answer to this question determines the shape of analysis and so also its starting point. Sequences of closely linked images are one essential element—Kunzle makes this the defining element of the comic strip: "(1) There must be a sequence of separate images; (2) There must be a preponderance of image over text; (3) The medium . . . must be . . . a mass medium; (4) The sequence must tell a story which is both moral and topical." The speech balloon, he argues, is not "a definitive ingredient of the comic strip."[4] Indeed, only occasionally in the examples from 1450 to 1825 assembled in his first volume do we find balloons. Rodolphe Töpffer, whose 1830s strips have a central place in Kunzle's second volume, does not use speech balloons; his stories contain so much writing that they are illustrated novellas. I admire Kunzle, a bold original scholar, for gathering these materials, without which my own philosophical study could not have been conceived. My difference here with him

3. The discussion of Kant, Sartre, and Husserl in Umberto Eco's account of Superman is one precedent (Umberto Eco, "The Myth of Superman," *Diacritics* 2, no. 1 [1972]: 16).

4. David Kunzle, *The Early Comic Strip: Narrative Strips and Picture Stories in the European Broadsheet from c. 1450 to 1825* (Berkeley and Los Angeles: University of California Press, 1973), 2–3. For a view closer to mine, see Robert C. Harvey, "The Aesthetics of the Comic Strip," *Journal of Popular Culture* 12 (1979): 640–52. I date the actual birth of the comic to 24 October 1897, when *The Yellow Kid* appeared; see Coulton Waught, *The Comics* (New York: Macmillan, 1947), fig. 2.

involves no disagreement about the historical facts but only a question of focus. Defining the comic strip as a narrative sequence with speech balloons, I believe that the examples in both of his books belong to the prehistory of comics, which emerge as a populist art form only around 1890. Most late Victorian visual narratives, stories told in a small number of pictures in narrative sequence, do not make systematic use of speech balloons as do true comics.[5] What Kunzle presents mostly are image sequences accompanied with words; the full integration of words into pictures in the speech balloon creates a new art, which raises novel aesthetic problems.

The speech balloon is a defining element of the comic because it establishes a word/image unity that distinguishes comics from pictures illustrating a text, like Tenniel's drawings for *Alice in Wonderland*. Tenniel's images, well suited to the story, are not an essential element of it. Speech balloons, because they are visible to the reader but do not lie within the picture space containing the depicted characters, distinguish comics from both old-master art and the seventeenth-century broadsheets presented by Kunzle. The speech balloon is a great philosophical discovery, a method of representing thought and words. Almost unknown before being exploited by comics artists, the speech balloon defines comics as neither a purely verbal nor a strictly visual art form, but as something radically new. The comic for Kunzle "is essentially a hybrid form, part verbal and part pictorial, the latter must be considered as its primary feature. . . . it cannot be dominated by text."[6] The problem he then faces is determining in individual cases whether image or text "carries the burden of the narrative." He assumes that a narrative must be either visual or verbal—and comics must thus be a mixture of the two. This I deny. Comics in my view are essentially a composite art: when they are successful, they have verbal and visual elements seamlessly combined.

The account I present of the crucial visual technology developed within comics by no means coincides with that presented in various admirable survey accounts, listed in my bibliography, from which I have learned a great deal. A full sociological analysis would need to deal with the great body of archival materials. But just as Descartes could philosophize using but a small selection of examples, so I identify the nature of comics by surveying a limited range of materials. I have little to say about

5. See Denis Gifford, *Victorian Comics* (London: George Allen & Unwin, 1976).
6. Kunzle, *The Early Comic Strip*, 2.

the distinctive styles of the individual comics artists. I focus closely on only Gary Larson and George Herriman, relatively marginal figures for the historian but especially revealing artists for my purposes. The examples illustrate my abstract philosophical reasoning.

A full sociological study, taking Kunzle's concerns into the present, could be a great contribution to cultural studies and would be a useful correction of the tendency of art historians to pay so little attention to an art form that attracts so much more public attention than any work displayed merely in museums. Although there have been various semiotic accounts of comics, no one has identified the specifically philosophical problems posed by comics. The theorizing developed in this book is closer to Gombrich's than to the semiotic theories that became fashionable in the American art world in the 1980s.

The history of representational art, as told by Vasari and Gombrich, is the story of the slow, often difficult discovery of the technology of visual representation. With comics, by contrast, already at the time of Giotto all of the necessary visual technology was available, but their development was possible only when there was a felt need for a readily accessible popular art. All the most important techniques of the comic strip were discovered quickly right at the start of its development. Since its origin, this art form has used these techniques to present stories. In focusing on these devices, the speech balloon and the narrative sequence, my account thus might be called a formal analysis—with the understanding that, as I show in Chapter 5, the form of comics places very real constraints on its content, on the kinds of stories that are most effectively told. The hypothesis governing my discussions of both balloons and narrative sequence is Gombrichian. We seek consistency, aiming to interpret all the elements in the visual field in some way that makes sense of them; and we are remarkably adaptable, willing to overlook minor inconsistencies so long as the words in the balloon can be attached to the image and the sequence of the images constitutes a meaningful narrative.

In the next to last chapter of *Art and Illusion*, Gombrich turns from the story of representation to the analysis of what he calls "the Experiment of Caricature," moving from an art devoted to visual discovery to this "illusion of life which can do without any illusion of reality." He seems ambivalent about how to analyze caricature. Sometimes he describes it as a special kind of representation: "[C]aricature becomes only a special case of what I have attempted to describe as the artist's test of success. All artistic discoveries are discoveries not of likenesses but of equivalences which enable us to see reality in terms of an image and an image in terms of reality." Just as Constable permits us to see his picture *Wivenhoe Park* as Wivenhoe Park because it looks like that estate, so a caricaturist enables us to see his image as depicting, in exaggerated ways, his subject. But that parallel takes account only of the conventional aspect of representation, not the way in which representations, unlike mere caricatures, really do look as much as possible like what they depict. This is why Gombrich associates Daumier with the political cartoonists and not "the French tradition of great art."[7] Representation making itself is emotionally neutral; caricature is essentially aggressive in its distortions.

Much of Gombrich's argument involves debate about the role of convention in representation. Perspective, he argues, against Erwin Panofsky, shows how things really appear—it is not merely a form of symbolic representation. He rejects the argument of Nelson Goodman that, because perspective is, strictly speaking, designed to "work" only under special viewing conditions, therefore it is not a scientific discovery. While Gombrich allows that there are conventional elements in representation, he claims that naturalistic pictures look like what they depict. He rejects semiotic theories of representation. In comics, almost everyone agrees, the speech balloon (but not the narrative sequence) is purely conventional. The concept of convention is elusive and subtle. For my present purposes, which are simpler than Gombrich's, a pictorial element is conventional if it would not be visible to someone standing within the picture space. If you could stand next to Donald Duck in a comic, you would see him, but not the words or thoughts in his speech balloon.

In the last chapter of *Art and Illusion*, "From Representation to Expression," the techniques associated with caricature lead forward to the abstract painting of Mondrian. I would describe the tradition of caricature in a different way, treating it as a natural extension of the concern of old-master and early modernist art with presenting verbal narratives in visual images. The style of my argumentation about comics is Gombrichian, but my art-historical narrative differs from his. We offer different, but not necessarily incompatible, accounts.

This book has three parts. Chapters 1 through 4 are devoted to identifying the nature of comics, Chapters 5 and 6 to explaining how they should be

---

7. E. H. Gombrich, *Art and Illusion* (Princeton: Princeton University Press, 1961), 336, 345, 252.

interpreted, and Chapter 7 to understanding their place in art's history. To interpret an art, we need to know its essence, its defining qualities; and with the art of comics, that requires understanding its origin. Once we know what kind of a thing the artwork is, we are prepared to explain its history. When comics are defined, we see how to interpret them and can recognize the character of their history.

This introduction has defined the comic as a closely grouped sequence of images using balloons. Chapter 1 discusses the origin of comics, explaining how caricatures involve imagining an implicit successor to a single image. That analysis prepares the way for two chapters focused on the comics' identifying features. Chapter 2 discusses speech and thought balloons, noting their origin in early Renaissance art and explaining why this rich visual resource was not systematically exploited until the development of comics. Chapter 3 then takes up the second defining characteristic, the closely linked succession of images. Comics use words and images—how do they bind them together? Chapter 4, dealing with that issue, explores the deep relation between comics and another kind of entity linking two such distinctly different elements, persons. Like literature, comics are narratives that are read; like paintings, comics are images that are viewed. And so a proper account must do justice to our experience of this unity, words-and-pictures. Here, finally, we come to the third and final essential feature of comics—their scale.

Having identified the essential qualities of comics, what then can we say about how they are interpreted? Chapter 5 takes up some relevant theories of text reading and picture viewing. This distinctive unity of comics reflects the identity of comics as a populist art form. Chapter 6 argues that such mass-culture images should be interpreted differently from old-master art. The meaning of a comic is determined not by the artist but by the audience; to interpret a comic we need to identify the ways in which it reflects the fantasies of its public.

Chapter 7, by showing how from the start the comic was essentially a posthistorical art, incapable of development, returns in a self-conscious way to my starting point. Once we fully understand the essence and history of comics, we are prepared to grasp their philosophical significance.

PART ONE

THE NATURE OF COMICS

CARICATURE; OR, REPRESENTING CAUSAL CONNECTION

'TIS ONLY *CAUSATION*, WHICH PRODUCES SUCH A CONNEXION, AS TO GIVE
US ASSURANCE FROM THE EXISTENCE OR ACTION OF ONE OBJECT, THAT
'TWAS FOLLOW'D OR PRECEDED BY ANY OTHER EXISTENCE OR ACTION.

—DAVID HUME, *A TREATISE OF HUMAN NATURE*

While working in my third-floor study, I can sometimes see the postman
coming along my quiet dead-end street. And when then I run downstairs,
I view the mail coming through the slot and hear my daughter's dog,
Brigston, rushing barking to defend the house. I understand what is happening at any given moment by relation to what happens earlier or later.
The mail appears in the door *because* the postman has arrived; Brigston
awakens *because* he hears the postman. I infer, as Hume noted, causal
connections between those pairs of events.

   This everyday experience tells something about how to look at an old-
master visual narrative. Viewing the *Nightwatch* in the Rijksmuseum, Amsterdam, I see the militiamen, arranged around the man at the center,
seeming to march forward toward me; "the impression of action . . . is so
persuasive that its admirers have long wondered whether the painting does
not depict some specific event."[1] That the painting is set on the far wall

---

1. Gary Schwartz, *Rembrandt: His Life, His Paintings* (New York: Viking, 1985), 210; see also
David Carrier, *Principles of Art History Writing* (University Park: The Pennsylvania State University Press, 1991), 197–200.

of a long room may encourage this illusion. Nowadays everyone is aware of the fallacies of interpreting old-master pictures as if they were photographs. Since artists of Rembrandt's time did not aspire to depict individual moments of ongoing actions, it would be anachronistic to identify moments before and after that instant they show. The general goal of such artists was to create a self-contained clear visual presentation. A photograph, because it is of the world, necessarily shows one of a sequence of moments. A painting, however naturalistic it may appear, does not have this relation to the visual world.[2]

In viewing some visual images, however, understanding the depicted scene does require imagining an earlier or later moment of the depicted action. To understand "Dropping the Pilot" (Fig. 1), a caricature discussed by Gombrich, we must see Bismarck, on the ship's ladder, as descending.[3] Someone who thought that Bismarck, walking backward, was preparing to ascend would give a quite fallacious reading, though one consistent with the visual evidence. Just as understanding one of Poussin's esoteric subjects requires knowing his iconography, so the correct interpretation of this image demands some background information about German politics. The viewer needs to know why Bismarck was represented as a pilot, dropped off by Wilhelm II. Such background knowledge is required also by Edward Gorey's images, where "the moment depicted is the moment of maximum drama, just *before* the effect of disaster."[4] Anticipating that next scene, our laughter expresses pleasure at our imagining of disaster.

Just as what Danto calls a narrative sentence makes reference to a later moment, so too must these pictures refer to some such later moment. "During the French revolution, the father of the author of *The Painter of Modern Life* renounced his priesthood." That description of Charles Baudelaire's father could only be understood in the 1860s, when *The Painter of Modern Life* was published. Narrative sentences that "refer to at least two time-separated events, and describe the earlier event," Danto argues, thus form the basis of historical explanations, which, by connect-

2. See Aaron Scharf, "Painting, Photography, and the Image of Movement," *Burlington Magazine* 10 (May 1962): 186–93, and William I. Homer, with John Talbot, "Eakins, Muybridge, and the Motion Picture Process," *Art Quarterly* 26, no. 2 (1963): 194–216.

3. See Gombrich, *Meditations on a Hobby Horse*, 131–32.

4. Karen Wilkin, "Mr. Earbrass Jots Down a Few Visual Notes: The World of Edward Gorey," in *The World of Edward Gorey*, by Clifford Ross and Karen Wilkin (New York: Abrams, 1996), 63; on the history of caricature, see Irving Lavin, "High and Low Before Their Time: Bernini and the Art of Social Satire," in *Modern Art and Popular Culture: Readings in High and Low*, ed. Kirk Varnedoe and Adam Gopnik (New York: Abrams, 1990), 8–51.

Fig. 1.   Tenniel, "Dropping the Pilot," *Punch*, 29 March 1890.

ing different moments, tell how the world changes.[5] Visual narratives, analogously, refer to at least two such separated moments. Hume asks how is it that we imagine connections between events. If causal connections are known only through experience, then why do we believe that one event inevitably is followed by another? Comics theorists ask a similar question. What experience gives us warrant to place an individual picture within such an imagined sequence?

How does representation work? Aestheticians and art historians invoke such diverse concepts as "art as illusion," "seeing in," and "seeing as" to describe the way that pigment on canvas or ink on paper represents.[6] Some think this a problem calling for an adequate technique of description; others believe that semiotic theorizing provides the key; and some, myself included, are inclined to suspect that experimental psychology provides the best analysis. Gombrich's account, in which the history of representation making is treated as a story of discovery, like that of scientific theorizing, has the great virtue of showing how this activity can be the source of a master narrative, linking together the concerns of European artists ranging from Cimabue to Constable and the Impressionists.[7]

How is it that from one isolated image we envisage earlier and later moments of an ongoing visual narrative? Caricatures pose this equally interesting but much less discussed question. Gombrich's argument that making successful representations involves projection may also help to explain caricature. The artist's aim is to enable the spectator to form some hypothesis about what is depicted. If that process is successful, the spectator's hypothesis matches the artist's intention, and that viewer sees illusionistically represented what the artist desired to depict. When, rather, the artist's image is visually ambiguous—capable of more than one plausible interpretation—then he or she has failed to communicate. Thus we understand many caricatures by forming some hypothesis about the previous or the next scene of the action.[8] Seeing the world, I know that it existed a moment earlier and will continue to exist. A picture shows

5. Arthur C. Danto, *Narration and Knowledge* (New York: Columbia University Press, 1985), 1.

6. Richard Wollheim, *Painting as an Art: The A. W. Mellon Lectures in the Fine Arts* (Princeton: Princeton University Press, 1987), chaps. 1–2.

7. See David Carrier, *Artwriting* (Amherst: University of Massachusetts Press, 1987), chaps. 1–2.

8. This argument is plausible quite apart from the ultimate critical judgment on Gombrich's theory of representation; unlike that account, a quasi-scientific testable theory, mine is a purely conceptual analysis.

only how things appear at one moment. Seeing a picture, I need not imagine that the depicted scene existed before and after the moment depicted. Many representations—still lifes, portraits, some landscapes—do not appear to define temporal sequences. Usually I do not imagine how the man portrayed got into his sitting position, or how he will stand up after the portrait is completed. What nowadays makes thinking about images as moments in narrative sequences so natural is movies. Just as, so it has been argued, the development of naturalistic representations made it possible to understand the first photographs, so perhaps long experience of caricatures and comics made the earliest films more accessible. "With a few rare exceptions, the comic strip gathered most of its basic expressive resources without recourse to the cinema, and often even before the later was born."[9]

Baudelaire gives a characteristically lively description of Daumier's great 1840 image *Le dernier bain* (Fig. 2): "Standing on the parapet of a quay and already leaning forward, so that his body forms an acute angle with the base from which it is parting company—like a statue losing its balance—a man is letting himself topple into the river. He must have really made up his mind, for his arms are calmly folded, and a huge pavingstone is attached to his neck with a rope."[10] In an instant, this poor man will be underwater dying, unseen by the placid fisherman on the opposite riverbank. Logically speaking, many other alternatives are visually consistent with what we see. The man could detach the weight; what appears a weight could rather be a container filled with feathers; he could fall safely into a boat; an angel or a person with a flying suit like the one worn by Buck Rogers could rescue him. But, just as a Constable landscape "works" as a representation because we inevitably see the small white mark as a house and not any number of other possible things, so Daumier's success involves creating an unambiguous picture. Even before reading the title, we are sure that this man is about to drown himself.

Many caricatures, of course, do not work this way.[11] But some carica-

9. Francis Lacassin, "The Comic Strip and Film Language," *Film Quarterly* 25, no. 4 (1972): 14. See also Donald Crafton, *Before Mickey: The Animated Film, 1898–1928* (Cambridge, Mass.: MIT Press, 1982).

10. Charles Baudelaire, *The Painter of Modern Life and Other Essays*, trans. Jonathan Mayne (London: Phaidon Press, 1964), 176; see Michele Hannoosh, *Baudelaire and Caricature: From the Comic to an Art of Modernity* (University Park: Pennsylvania State University Press, 1992), 139–40.

11. In some special cases, a picture that appears an isolated still scene can, when properly analyzed, be revealed as essentially belonging to a narrative sequence. The drawing of his dream

tures are protocomics because understanding them requires imagining a later moment of the action. In his analysis of representation, Gombrich argues that projection can be understood by knowing what background information we bring to the picture. With caricatures, analogously, how we interpret depends upon such knowledge. In the caricature of Bismarck, we require information about German history; in the Daumier, common-sense knowledge about the effects of gravity. These two caricatures are in this way ideologically neutral: whether you admire or detest Bismarck, whatever your views on suicide, you will see these images the same way.

Gombrich gives Rodolphe Töpffer's caricatures a key role in the history of modernism: "It needs the detachment of an enlightened nineteenth-century humorist to play with the magic of creation, to make up these playful doodles, and to question them for their character and soul as if they were real creatures."[12] Earlier, he suggests, it was not possible to handle aggressive images in this detached way. Caricature is inherently an art of exaggeration. The Neoplatonic tradition involves creating ideal beauty, finding that perfection realized only imperfectly in actual individuals; caricature (and the comic) involves deformation. Engraved images of modern life, Baudelaire observes, "can be translated either into beauty or ugliness; in one direction, they become caricatures, in the other, antique statues."[13] Manet painted modern beauty; Daumier had an altogether different concern. There are many obscene caricatures, and a great deal of sex in comics; but the characters are never ideal enough to be beautiful.[14]

As Baudelaire explained, Louis Philippe caricatured as a pear is a classic example of visual aggression.[15] "Philipon . . . wanted to prove . . . that nothing was more innocent than that prickly and provoking pear. . . . in the very presence of the court, he drew a series of sketches of which the first exactly reproduced the royal physiognomy, and each successive one, drawing further and further away from the primary image, approached

---

by Freud's patient the Wolf Man may be an example; see Whitney Davis, *Replications: Archaeology, Art History, Psychoanalysis* (University Park: Pennsylvania State University Press, 1996), chap. 11.

12. Gombrich, *Art and Illusion*, 342.

13. Baudelaire, *The Painter of Modern Life*, 2.

14. See Bob Adelman, with Art Spiegelman, Richard Merkin, and Madeline Kripke, *Tijuana Bibles: Art and Wit in America's Forbidden Funnies, 1930s–1950s* (New York: Simon & Schuster, 1997).

15. Baudelaire, *The Painter of Modern Life*, 172. See Elise K. Kenney and John M. Merriman, *The Pear: French Graphic Arts in the Golden Age of Caricature*, exhibition catalogue (South Hadley, Mass.: Mount Holyoke College Art Museum, 1991).

Fig. 2.   Daumier, *Le dernier bain*, 1840.

ever closer to the fatal goal—the *pear!*" When, in the course of writing *High Art: Charles Baudelaire and the Origins of Modernism*, I came to Baudelaire's essays on caricature, I was pleased that Michele Hannoosh's recent book dealt so thoroughly with this topic.[16] My own approach, providing a philosophically plausible reconstruction of Baudelaire's ideas rather than merely setting them in historical context, was not easy to extend to caricature. Hannoosh's admirably detailed discussion of the caricaturists discussed by Baudelaire provides a very full and convincing statement of the historical context of his thinking, but has little to say about the application of his ideas to present-day caricature. That is unsurprising, for this part of his aesthetic theory is grounded in highly traditional Catholic ideals.

Much (but not all) of Baudelaire's *Painter of Modern Life* can be read as a manifesto for modernist art, a prophecy of the tradition of art depicting urban consumer society, a tradition running from Manet and the Impressionists to Andy Warhol, the other Pop artists, and their successors in the 1990s.[17] On the Essence of Laughter, like Baudelaire's account of Delacroix, seems centered on ideas now essentially of historical interest.[18] Baudelaire proclaims that our pleasure in laughter shows the importance of original sin. We laugh because we are sinners: "It is certain that human laughter is intimately linked with the accident of an ancient Fall. . . . In the earthly paradise . . . joy did not find its dwelling in laughter" (149–50). Christ experienced anger and tears; but "in the eyes of One who has all knowledge and all power, the comic does not exist" (149). It seems obviously difficult to extract his claims from this essentially theological context. When most modern-day unbelievers have great difficulty taking such claims literally, what remains of Baudelaire's theory of caricature?[19]

What then has caused me to reconsider this way of thinking has been more recent study of a contemporary caricaturist whose images exemplify this Baudelairean theory of humor in absolutely uncanny ways. Although in the 1980s Gary Larson became much more famous than anyone known only within the art world, his caricatures have not inspired much com-

16. Hannoosh, *Baudelaire and Caricature*.

17. A different approach is provided by Gérald Froidevaux, *Baudelaire: Représentation et modernité* (Paris: José Corti, 1989), chap. 5, "La caricature ou l'affirmation négative du beau."

18. Baudelaire, *The Painter of Modern Life*, 147–65; further references are incorporated directed into the text.

19. As Paul Benacerraf has pointed out to me, even on its own level this theory has obvious problems. Suppose that we all are fallen. Still, not everyone laughs at the same jokes. Appeal to our shared fallen condition cannot explain why we respond differently to jokes.

mentary, so far as I know, by art critics.[20] This is surprising, for his extraordinarily inventive images tell us a great deal about American culture of that era.[21] Larson employs repeated, even obsessive, development of a few central concerns; for every example I cite, many similar ones could easily be provided.

Totally apolitical—apart from his passionate support for animal rights—Larson hates change, which he thinks always brings disaster. Taking almost all his subjects from lower- or middle-class white American life, but not a chauvinist, his only significant foreign settings are African jungles, the Arctic, and rivers inhabited by headhunters. Borderlines between city and country, humans and animals, are blurred: deer are hunted in their own living rooms; dogs steal family cars; animals take photos on vacation and appear on quiz shows. Larson loves endless mindless repetition—people in hell doing five million leg lifts or discovering that cold fronts never arrive, and disasters that befall those stupid enough to eat potato chips or buy tropical fish in the desert. (Heaven is of less interest to him than hell.) He shows petty theft, minor crime, and, occasionally, homicide; menacing ocean scenes hold a special attraction for him. He adores sharks.

Larson's archaeologists are doomed never to learn about the past, his anthropologists to understand nothing of the "natives" they study. His animals mimic humans doing stupid things. Larson's world is oddly asexual in a preadolescent-male way. He loves toilet humor and human-animal couples, not as illustrations of bestiality but as just another variety of dumbness. His women would just as soon be married to animals—and why not, when all people are so stupid? Apart from such normal fascinations as dog-cat battles, his odd obsessions include cross-dressing cowboys, men with peg legs, and—what does this mean?—the erotic significance of chickens. His stupid, sadistic, and dysfunctional characters enjoy their lives. Gravely serious academic commentators have written much about "postmodernism" and the end of history. Larson's immense popularity—is there anyone who really dislikes his work?—shows that, at some level, very many people suspect that progress is finished. It is hard to imagine him showing the triumph of virtue.

---

20. But see Bill Berkson, *Homage to George Herriman,* exhibition catalogue (San Francisco: Campbell-Thiebaud Gallery, 1997), and MaLin Wilson, "DemoKrazy in the American West," *Art Issues,* September/October 1997, 24–27.

21. My subject is Larson the cartoonist as revealed in his work, not the person, whom I have never met.

The man at the blackboard who has discovered "the purpose of the universe"—an elaborate equation he works on sums up to zero—summarizes Larson's worldview. Living in a run-down universe can be fun. Scientists who play games instead of doing research, pilots who cannot read instrument-panel dials, a musician who tries to perform with only one cymbal: Larson's characters are happily, hopelessly incompetent. He really has only this one major theme, disaster. This is why encountering his pictures one by one in the newspaper was more fun than looking at the collections of his art. Humor of this sort is only occasionally a central concern in old-master art.[22] Unfunny paintings, calling for knowledge of esoteric texts, give their interpreters the sense that they are smart. Larson's cartoons make you feel as stupid as the characters he loves to depict; temporarily imagining being stupid, he shows, can be fun. Or as he puts it, quoting Mel Brooks: "Tragedy is when I cut my finger. Comedy is when you walk into an open sewer and die."[23]

The essence of such humor, Baudelaire claims, is to "to produce in the spectator, or rather the reader, a joy in his own superiority" (164). Seeing Larson's idiotic characters, we recognize our own modest superiority. I would never let my daughter's dog drive while I hung out the car window like a dog. A farmer meets extraterrestrials who are walking hands: "Inadvertently, Roy dooms the entire earth to annihilation when, in an attempt to be friendly, he seizes their leader by the head and shakes vigorously."[24] Why is Roy's action funny? Few people really desire that our planet be destroyed. And yet, the idea that it might be destroyed by aliens so dumb as to be offended by Roy is amusing. We laugh, flattered to be reminded that we are not as stupid as people who read manuals about snake identification while poisonous snakes bite them, or aliens who come all the way to Earth to steal chickens. Responding aesthetically, we enjoy imagining disaster. It may seem odd to speak of "an aesthetic response," for all of Larson's figures, even Jackie Onassis, are hopelessly ugly. And yet, what lucky people! Their ugliness does not disturb them, for they are found desirable by others. When "the elephant man meets a buffalo gal," they find each other ravishing.[25] In his apolitical way, Larson shows the problems with belief in the superiority of your own species.

22. But see Paul Barolsky, *Infinite Jest: Wit and Humor in Italian Renaissance Art* (Columbia: University of Missouri Press, 1978).

23. Gary Larson, *The Prehistory of "The Far Side": A Tenth Anniversary Exhibit* (Kansas City, Mo.: Andrews & McMeel, 1989), 5.

24. Gary Larson, *The Far Side Gallery 3* (Kansas City, Mo.: Andrews & McMeel, 1988), 78.

25. Gary Larson, *The Far Side Gallery 4* (Kansas City, Mo.: Andrews & McMeel, 1989), 109.

Fascinated by religion, Larson is seriously skeptical of its claims. His characters frequently are scientists or inventors, but he rejects belief in technological progress entirely. It is surprising that nerds, one of his great subjects, love him. Everyone in his pictures looks old, even the children— they have no future. Bad as it presently is, our world could be even worse: that assertion is funny because we postmoderns fear that it might be true. Perhaps this is why technocrats seem especially to enjoy his work—this worry must be an occupational hazard for them. Larson appeals to those who don't much like modern art. When he shows Leonardo da Vinci learning to draw from a matchbook advertisement, you cannot but feel his populist ambivalence about high culture.

Need you be a closet sadist to laugh at Larson's fat woman calling for her dog to run into a blocked door, "Here, Fifi! C'mon! . . . Faster, Fifi!"?[26] When Amnesty International objected to his scenes of torture— "Congratulations Bob Torturer of the Month" reads the slogan behind three bound victims—he said: "[T]his group has at least raised my consciousness to this problem."[27] Like cat lovers who objected to showing the dog's tying up the new cat, these critics blur the line between appearance and reality. No doubt we all do that in responding to caricatures, but without some such temporary suspension of disbelief, cartoon art would be impossible. Could a man in a slowly sinking rubber life raft be watching a portable TV? Might a time machine run out of gas, leaving its inventor stranded among dinosaurs? Would deer tie up a hunter, leaving the hunting license stuck in his mouth? If you think too much, Larson's images cannot "come off." To understand his art, you must enjoy momentarily being stupid.

Comedy—this is the true cliché—is an inherently conservative artistic genre. It shows that nothing changes. You cannot "tell" a Matisse, for his art is essentially visual; but you can usually "tell" a Larson, for mostly his conceptions are verbal. What Baudelaire calls our "double nature" (165) consists in the capacity to enjoy imagining people being injured in disasters while ourselves remaining safe. God and advanced intelligences from other planets are no smarter than humans in Larson's anthropomorphic world, where the sun rises and sets, run by a man who operates a switch. Aliens intelligent enough to operate flying saucers crash because a bee enters their spacecraft or because they get too close to the Statue of Lib-

26. Gary Larson, *The Far Side Gallery 2* (Kansas City, Mo.: Andrews & McMeel, 1986), 9.
27. Larson, *The Prehistory of "The Far Side*," 164.

erty. Even God is humanly stupid: he dials the wrong phone number; discovers that snakes are easy to construct; and when but only a child—who are His parents?—tries to make a chicken in his room.

Almost all Larsons are absurdly easy to interpret. (When it takes effort to understand his images, as in some few he himself analyzes, then he fails.) Very often commentary treats modernist museum art as personal expression, the artist's choice of subjects understood in relation to his or her politics and private life. When Larson shows scenes that almost everyone understands immediately, asking about his personal beliefs is irrelevant. Many accounts of populist culture, growing out of Marxist tradition, propose to see through such images; today this condescending procedure is no longer satisfying. No doubt Larson expresses a childhood that his biographer might describe. But insofar as we value a Larson for what it tells us about our collective desires, fantasies, and fears, such analysis is essentially irrelevant. What constitutes the interpretation of a Larson is laughter. In thus interpreting, we learn about ourselves and our culture.

Larson almost always has a very simple iconography. Two men in a disheveled room peel open the venetian blind: "Roommates Elvis and Salman Rushdie sneak a quick look at the outside world."[28] To understand Larson's images you need only know about the culture's most famous heroes: Einstein (the would-be basketball player), Picasso, Superman, and people in the headlines, like the once notorious hijacker D. B. Cooper. "Only a one-liner"—what visual artist wants to be told that once you have "gotten it," there is nothing more to be said about his or her works? But Larson's entire oeuvre consists of but the pleasure of imagining disaster, which is perhaps why he retired early on—he seems to have been a one-theme artist.[29]

For a long time, Baudelaire's unoriginal theory of humor seemed to me obviously implausible.[30] Finding Baudelaire's odd antitheology absurd, it seemed a waste of time to analyze his argumentation. Some modern caricaturists play with Baudelairean pleasure in doing evil.[31] Edward Gorey's

28. Gary Larson, *The Far Side Gallery 5* (Kansas City, Mo.: Andrews & McMeel, 1995), 23.

29. His work has some affinities with Thurber's, but otherwise it is hard to cite art-historical sources for Larson's art. He has, in obviously ironical ways, described his childhood sources of his art; see Gary Larson, *The Curse of Madame "C": A Far Side Collection* (Kansas City, Mo.: Andrews & McMeel, 1994).

30. Larson's one exercise in Baudelairean Satanism, the scene of Christ, risen from the grave, wondering "what time it is. . . . I feel like I've been dead for three days" (Larson, *The Prehistory of "The Far Side,"* 105), is, as he notes, not funny.

31. See David Carrier, "Introduction: Baudelaire's Metaphysics," in *High Art: Charles Baudelaire and the Origins of Modernism* (University Park: Pennsylvania State University Press, 1996).

scenes of children's disasters belong to this somewhat precious self-consciously camp tradition. But unlike Gorey, Larson is genuinely popular. Baudelaire's irony, Hannoosh argues, implies that his account of humor should be interpreted, not as merely false, but metaphorically, as an ironizing that itself is "an example of comic art in the best sense."[32] To enjoy such visual jokes, we must pretend to take the doctrine seriously, while knowing that it is false, and not simply reject Baudelaire's theology or take it to be true. This kind of play is very naturally associated with Larson's caricatures, which are funny only for the viewer who can pretend to accept something like his view of sin. If you find Christian morality absurd (or offensive), then you can hardly make sense of joking scenes set in hell; if you believe the wicked are punished, then the idea that this hot place might temporarily be cooled by a boiler failure cannot be funny.

Only some of Larson's scenes play with theology in this way, but this attitude can be suggestively generalized to explain how he thinks of his nonreligious subjects. Very frequently he shows animals behaving like, or being mistaken for, humans. Denying that human beings are inherently different from animals, he thus touches upon religious tradition. To imagine that a cat could kill a bird by blowing up its cage, that a dog would play ventriloquist to a cat sitting on his knee, or that rowers on a slave ship could be entertained by a pianist playing *Row, Row, Row Your Boat:* this requires taking something like a former believer's attitude toward religion. What is comic for Larson is any situation that can be called absurd because it is neither simply the way things are nor just impossible to imagine. To speak in Baudelaire's terms, we laugh because "an artist is only an artist on the condition that he is a double man"—because "it is perfectly true that he knows what he is doing; but he also knows that the essence of this type of the comic is that it should appear to be unaware of itself" (164).

Frequently, modern attitudes toward theological tradition embody this essentially comic attitude. How funny it would be, a secular person can think, were such preposterous beliefs correct. A dying atheist who finds him or herself in hell ought to be ready to laugh. In *High Art* I argue that Baudelaire's general aesthetic includes two very different accounts: a traditionally oriented way of thinking and an anticipation of radically original art of the city—a compromise expressed in his passionate admiration for both Delacroix and Guys. What makes his theorizing hard to

---

32. Hannoosh, *Baudelaire and Caricature*, 283.

grasp, I claim, is that it presents both these very different approaches without any attempt at synthesis. The same could be said about his theory of caricature, which both looks backward historically to religious tradition and, by treating that way of thinking ironically, expresses the skepticism associated with modernist secularization. When we laugh at Larson's images, we both take seriously religious ideas and refuse to take literally those out-of-date ways of thinking; to describe this situation in Hannoosh's ironical terms, the very doubleness of our divided nature appears when viewing one such image.

Why do we laugh at Larsons? *High Art* draws attention to the general way in which Baudelaire follows the tradition in which interpreters understand a picture by "moving it," envisaging the next moment of a scene. The difficulty of modernist visual art, I argue, is that insofar as it fails to indicate what will happen next, it threatens to be indecipherable. Larson's humor very often depends upon a viewer's expectation about how thus "to move" images. (This he probably learned from comics, in which that next scene is actually depicted.) Presented with one moment of an ongoing action, we imagine disaster in the next scene. As he explains, his images are funniest when, only implying "what is about to happen," they thereby heighten "the tension."[33] "Don't be alarmed folks. . . . He's completely harmless unless something startles him."[34] Imagining the next scene, when the door of a crowded elevator will close on this "harmless" lion's tail, is funny. Why do we project the next scene thus? There is, after all, nothing to prevent us from imagining that disaster is averted.

A model of the way we "move" such pictures is provided by the great Larson in which a hapless man walks unknowingly to face a sniper: "Misunderstanding his employees' screams of 'Simmons has lost his marbles,' Mr. Wagner bursts from his office for the last time."[35] Imagining the next moment when Wagner will be murdered, we laugh. (Is this Wagner the composer? The Germanic name may be part of the hostile joke.) The wordplay with the phrase "losing your marbles" is essential. Were the caption to read, "Misunderstanding his employees' screams of 'Simmons has a gun,' Mr. Wagner bursts from his office for the last time," the image would not be funny. That we seemingly freely choose the next scene reveals our double nature. We enjoy cruelly imagining disaster. There is

33. Larson, *The Prehistory of "The Far Side,"* 136.
34. Gary Larson, *The Far Side Gallery* (Kansas City, Mo.: Andrews & McMeel, 1984), 192.
35. Larson, *The Far Side Gallery 4,* 142.

nothing to prevent us from supposing that the sniper throws down his weapon or that Wagner, recognizing the danger, does not come forward. Unlike Baudelaire, I hesitate to draw theological conclusions. That we gain aesthetic pleasure from Larsons does not show that in life we, his admirers, are sadists. Perhaps one benevolent function of such art is to permit us to discharge our inevitable hostility in harmless ways. This disaster we imagine is not, so we hypocritically think, really our fault—we only pretend that it seems inevitable. Caught (in ways Freud analyzed in his discussion of verbal joking) in the pleasure of aggressive play, we would prefer to imagine Wagner's death. Such pictures are what Danto calls enthymemes, visual syllogisms with an obvious missing premise, which the reader must supply. This reader "is not, as a passive auditor, told what to put there; he must find that out and put it there himself."[36] Reasoning thus, we both acknowledge aggressive fantasy and disavow any such intention. Deceiving ourselves, we pretend that it is not our malice but only Larson's situation that inevitably will bring about disaster.

36. I borrow from Arthur C. Danto, *The Transfiguration of the Commonplace: A Philosophy of Art* (Cambridge, Mass.: Harvard University Press, 1981), 170, on the rhetoric of visual images.

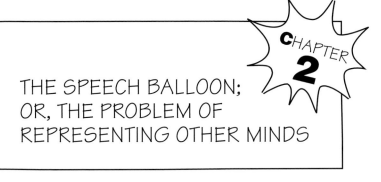

THE SPEECH BALLOON; OR, THE PROBLEM OF REPRESENTING OTHER MINDS

CHAPTER 2

IF WE ARE TO SAY THAT THERE IS A FORMAL OBJECT OF THOUGHT WE
MUST SAY THAT IT IS: ANYTHING WHATEVER.

—ANTHONY KENNY, *ACTION, EMOTION, AND WILL*

In the early 1970s, under the spell of Adrian Stokes, the first art writer who influenced me deeply, I took the long bus trip east from Arezzo up into the mountains of the Marches to Urbino to see Piero della Francesca's *Flagellation*. Part of the special fascination of that famous painting is its relative inaccessibility. Once in Urbino, even the art tourist pressed for time cannot avoid walking through the courtyard by Luciano Laurana, in which, as Stokes writes,[1] "there are variations in its surface, mostly of colour or tone, that the eye with one flash discovers coherent, so that perceptions of succession belonging to any estimate of length or height or density, retire in favour of a feeling that here you witness a concatenation, a simultaneity, that the object is *exposed* to you, all of it all at once." Such trips made me very aware of the contrast between the experience of standing before a much discussed painting, immediately present to that artifact, and reading the literature about it. Piero is challenging to write

---

1. Adrian Stokes, *The Critical Writings of Adrian Stokes* (London: Thames & Hudson, 1978), 1:134.

about in part because all his works can never be gathered in exhibition and therefore the connoisseur, who goes from Urbino to Arezzo, Berlin, Boston, Florence, London, Manhattan, Milan, Monterchi, Oxford, Perugia, Sansepolcro, Rimini, Venice, and Williamstown, must rely heavily upon memory. The art writer looks at pictures and reads commentary on them, and the difficult task then is to relate images and words properly. Writing when far away from the original images, working only from reproductions, is difficult. The traditional ekphrasis reflects that situation. It "is written in the past tense" and involves the art writer's "freely and openly using his mind. . . . what a description will tend to represent best is thought after seeing a picture."[2] Unlike old-master paintings, comic strips can be written about while being viewed.

Seeking consistency, Gombrich explains, we expect every picture element to contribute to the meaning of the image, and so read words within the frame as represented elements. This is why premodernist narrative painters, for all of their resourcefulness, did not often employ balloons, which they knew from broadsides; such alien elements within the picture space inevitably seemed unaesthetic intrusions. This well-entrenched word/image distinction is a deconstructionist's dream, for identifying a rigid, apparently uncrossable dividing line is to beg that it be crossed. Balloons, "the word made image," as one French semiotic commentator calls them, neither purely verbal nor just pictorial, but both one and the other at once, bridge the word/image gap.[3]

Ralph Hodgon has been identified as the first artist to put speech within the frame, using an ingenious compromise, explanatory placards.[4] In 1906, Winsor McCay realized that the narrative at the bottom of his panels "was an irrelevant gloss on the action."[5] Removing it, he "made Little Nemo into a more purely visual narrative art form," the modern comic strip. The comics artist Will Eisner offers a challenging naturalistic interpretation of the balloon:[6]

> Steam from warm air expelled during conversation can be seen.
> It is logical to combine that which is heard within that which is seen resulting in a visualized image of the act of speaking.

2. Michael Baxandall, *Patterns of Intention: On the Historical Explanation of Pictures* (New Haven: Yale University Press, 1985), 4.

3. Pierre Fresnault-Druelle, *La bande dessinée: L'univers et les techniques de quelques "comics" d'expression française* (Paris: Hachette, 1972), chap. 2.

4. Gifford, *Victorian Comics*, 24.

5. M. Thomas Inge, *Comics as Culture* (Jackson: University Press of Mississippi, 1990), 33.

6. Will Eisner, *Comics and Sequential Art* (Tamarac, Fla.: Poorhouse Press, 1985), 26.

Perhaps some early cartoonist was influenced by seeing the steam people exhaled when speaking in cold weather. Italians call the comic a "fumetto," a "puff of smoke," an elegant synecdoche that identifies at once both the balloon and the entire panel, picture plus balloon. But since exhaled steam does not contain written words, it is hard to see how this observation by itself could yield a conception of the comics balloon. Painted representations of people look like people; words in speech balloons are intended to be heard by readers who know the language in which they are written. The speech balloon must therefore be purely conventional.

Words in balloons cannot be placed within this apparently inescapable word/image binary opposition, for they are neither entirely within the picture space nor outside it. When "an inner contact between picture and script" is not established, "the picture remains a cumbersome alien body in the book."[7] Words in pictures are "semantic enclaves"—they are "signs of a different kind from a different system than signs of which the main body of that work of art consists."[8] Imagine a theater with a soundproof glass wall between actors and audience, and with the spectators reading the dialogue from supertitles. Seeing a play in such a theater would be like reading comics.

Awareness not just of the words balloons contain but also of their purely visual qualities is part of our experience of comics. We treat the balloons neither purely as holes in the picture nor as things depicted. McCay was skilled at choosing where best to place the balloon dialogues, which can occupy a rather large portion of the entire picture space. The style of type employed for the words is also significant; the typeface in 1940s *Batman* and *Superman,* as much a part of its period style as the cars or planes depicted, is visibly different from that in the Tintin translations or the older styles of script employed in *Little Nemo* and *Krazy Kat.* The lettering of Edward Gorey and Roz Chast in their comics is as stylistically individual as their narratives. (Chast, unlike Gorey, often uses balloons, one obvious indication that her work, more than his, is set in our contemporary world.) Normally reprinting a novel doesn't require duplicating the type of the first edition. But modernizing the type in a cartoon would change that artwork.

Words in balloons, unlike depicted architecture or furniture, usually don't obstruct the characters. Balloon words are neither in nor outside

---

7. Otto Pächt, *Book Illumination in the Middle Ages: An Introduction,* trans. Kay Davenport (New York: Oxford University Press, 1984), 129.

8. Mieczyslaw Wallis, "Inscriptions in Paintings," *Semiotica* 9 (1973): 1.

the picture; like thoughts, sometimes said to be located "inside your head," they have no position in space. According to Descartes, we cannot know another person's mind directly; we can only infer thoughts from their outward expression in words and gesture. "A science of language must recover the *natural*—that is, the simple and original—relationships between speech and writing, that is, between an inside and an outside."[9] The possibility of skepticism arises, for there is a potential gap between the indirect ways in which I know your thoughts and the immediate intuition in which they are revealed to you. Balloons reveal what a philosopher of mind might dream of, that another person's thoughts be displayed indubitably and transparently. As often happens, when dreams are fulfilled, the result is unexpected, even disconcerting. What in the picture was presented as speech or thoughts becomes, in our space, words. These thoughts are revealed, not to any character within the strip, but only to us viewers who stand outside. The balloon, like Descartes's pineal gland, thus links things in two different worlds; we spectators are set apart from the depicted characters, as is the mind from the body. Comics do not merely duplicate the functions of the older system of expression, but add to them in essentially new ways. Poussin can have us imagine his characters' speech by depicting their gestures, but displaying concealed thought was normally beyond his powers.

Literature is an allographic art. The physical way in which a text is presented—the typeface, color of paper, and binding—does not usually constitute an aesthetically relevant feature of a novel. The note about typography found at the back of Alfred A. Knopf fiction marks that publisher's unusually sensitive concern with these extraliterary qualities of its books. When we read the contents of balloons, our first concern may be with the meaning of the words they contain. But since comics are also a visual art, we are concerned as well with the strictly visual qualities of balloons. We contrast elegantly shaped and awkward-looking balloons and are aware of the visual qualities of the chosen type, which we read in the ways we read handwriting for signs of someone's character. "[Saul] Steinberg was among the first to recognize that the properties and machinery of the comics—the onomatopoeic exclamation, the dialogue balloon, the bubbled line that symbolizes thought—had become a modern decorative order."[10] He has aesthetic concern for words as well as images.

9. Jacques Derrida, *Of Grammatology*, trans. Gayatri Chakravorty Spivak (Baltimore: Johns Hopkins University Press, 1976), 35.

10. Kirk Varnedoe and Adam Gopnik, *High and Low: Popular Culture and Modern Art* (New York: Museum of Modern Art, 1990), 190.

The balloon can contain any image combined with any words; it may even be completely blank, showing that a character has no thoughts.[11] Balloons in Robert Crumb's *Head Comix* contain not only words but allegorical pictures; question marks and exclamation points; movements across completely separate balloons, as when a heart in one character's balloon is shattered by a gun fired from another's balloon; meaningless words; eyeballs; and elaborate visually self-sufficient fantasy scenes.[12] Within one Gary Larson cartoon, we can have several languages, a man speaking to a duck in German, Spanish, French, and finally in "Duckese," "Quack? Quack!"[13] Tintin's dog, Snowy, thinks in human languages, but only speaks to say "Wooah! Wooah!" Gary Larson's version of this device, contrasting what a person says to a dog, "Okay, Ginger! I've had it!" with what the dog hears, "blah blah GINGER blah," is less elegant, for the need to add a caption below acknowledges his failure to come up with a specifically visual way of presenting this thought.[14]

Balloons can contain vivid assertion (words in capitals) or transparent grandiloquence, as in the "ornate" typography Walt Kelly gives to the flimflam of P. T. Bridgeport; emphatic puzzlement, as when Tintin's balloon contains "!" and "?" in color;[15] language different from the primary language of the comic, like the odd "English" of *Krazy Kat;* underlined thoughts, by way of emphasis;[16] unspoken thoughts when a series of bubbles joins balloon to the character; musical notes in *Peanuts;* thoughts in dreams, when the figure to whom the balloon is attached is asleep; balloons within balloons, representing thoughts of a character attributing thoughts to other characters;[17] hearts and broken hearts, showing love and falling out of love; thoughts in pictures, when the balloon contains depictions of things desired or imagined;[18] wish fulfillment, as when in a Larson a crow's dream is represented with that bird coming upon a flattened elephant;[19] words expressing the sense of the spoken words —"(sigh) and best of all. . ."—or increasing in size to indicate increase in

11. Ibid., 217.

12. Robert Crumb, *R. Crumb's Head Comix* (New York: Simon & Schuster, 1988), unpaginated.

13. Larson, *The Far Side Gallery,* 92.

14. Ibid., 30.

15. Hergé, *The Red Sea Sharks* (Boston: Little, Brown, 1970), 4.

16. *Batman Dailies: Volume I, 1943–1944* (Princeton, Wis.: Kitchen Sink Press, 1990), 46.

17. For analysis of an example, see David Carrier, "He Dreams She Dreams of Him," in *Puzzles About Art: An Aesthetics Casebook,* ed. M. Battin, J. Fisher, R. Moore, and A. Silvers (New York: St. Martins Press, 1989), 77–78.

18. Hergé, *The Red Sea Sharks,* 30.

19. Larson, *The Prehistory of "The Far Side,"* 243.

volume;[20] ellipses to show hesitation; upside-down balloons in *Li'l Abner* when a character is hanging upside down (Fig. 3);[21] backward balloons in *Krazy Kat* for a crab who walks and talks backward and for the other characters when they talk to that crab;[22] and whispered words, audible to a character but unreadable by the viewer.

We are amazingly flexible at making image/word connections. Once, when *The Far Side* was printed next to *Dennis the Menace*, the captions were accidentally switched, improving (so Larson jestingly suggests) both cartoons. Readers were able to relate the pictures to the captions below.[23] Even when the words do not seem to fit the image, we seek some connection between them. Viewing a comic, our expectation is that the unit, text plus picture, is comprehensible. Do we think in words, as some recent philosophers claim, or in pictures? Comics don't answer that question, for balloons employ both verbal and visual means to represent thought, without characterizing thought in itself. Comics thus solve the problem of

Fig. 3.   Al Capp, *Li'l Abner*, detail, 1935. *Li'l Abner Dailies, Volume One: 1934–1936* (Princeton, Wis.: Kitchen Sink Press, 1988), 227. Li'l Abner © and ™ Capp Enterprises, Inc. Published by Kitchen Sink Press. Used with permission.

20. *Batman Dailies: Volume I*, 77.

21. Al Capp, *Li'l Abner Dailies, Volume One: 1934–1936* (Princeton, Wis.: Kitchen Sink Press, 1988), 227.

22. George Herriman, *The Komplete Kat Komics* (Forestville, Calif.: Eclipse Books, 1991), 8:45.

23. Larson, *The Prehistory of "The Far Side,"* 127.

other minds only at the cost of dissolving it. The balloon must be attached to something, whether person or alien, capable of thinking. Car tires go "Screech" and bombs "Boom!" but only beings capable of thought, like the great Saul Steinberg's chair dreaming of being a rocking horse, can have balloons attached to them.[24]

Words in a balloon usually are in the present tense, like dialogue in a novel. We see the character and learn what he is saying or thinking. The normal way to take us into the past is a flashback, the characters represented speaking or thinking in the present tense at what we know to be an earlier time.[25] Adding other languages allows for still more complex effects. In Japanese comics, "when a Chinese person appears . . . his dialogue balloon is liable to show he is Chinese by using many vertically arranged ideograms—for this is what written Chinese text actually looks like. If a Westerner is speaking, his dialogue balloons may be written horizontally in an angular *katayana*—a script usually reserved for foreign derived words."[26] The background on which the depicted scene and balloons are placed does not always have a passive role, but may enter into the narrative. When balloons come from the picture edge, as in the wake-up call given for Little Nemo (Fig. 4), we read them as spoken by some character not visible within the picture frame. Normally the balloon, like the frame, is a passive element, but in a 1905 strip, *Little Sammy Sneeze* by Winsor McCay, a sneeze shatters the frame, which in the last image falls to rest on a character.[27] And in one *Peanuts* cartoon, the balloon falls from sleepy Snoopy's head, landing with a "klunk!"[28] When several characters are speaking or thinking, the left-to-right and top-to-bottom order of balloons determines the order of reported thoughts.

Comics generally are absolutely unambiguous, for they need to be read quickly. When but one character is shown in each image, then the words are that person's thoughts. In such cases, we may speak of an implicit balloon. Cartoons with implicit balloons differ from David Kunzle's pretwentieth-century examples, in which the words, attached below the pic-

24. Harold Rosenberg, *Saul Steinberg*, exhibition catalogue (New York: Alfred A. Knopf, 1978), unpaginated.

25. But in one, Larson animals speak in the past tense; Gary Larson, *The Chickens Are Restless* (Kansas City, Mo.: Andrews & McMeel, 1993), 71.

26. Frederik L. Schodt, *Manga! Manga! The World of Japanese Comics* (Tokyo: Kodansha International, 1983), 23.

27. Inge, *Comics as Culture*, 31.

28. Robert Benayoun, *Vroom, Tchac, Zowie: Le ballon dans la bande dessinée* (Paris: André Balland, 1968), 81.

Fig. 4.   Winsor McCay, *Little Nemo*, detail, 1907. As published in *The Complete Little
          Nemo in Slumberland*, ed. Richard Marschall (Ardsley, Pa.: Remco
          Worldservice Books, 1989).

ture, are thoughts or speech of characters. In his 1605/6 Dutch print *How
Various English Noblemen Decide to Destroy the King and the Whole Parliament with Gunpowder* (Fig. 5), the words merely accompany the picture,
without entering the image.[29] The burden of the action is carried by narrative outside the image. A revealing Larson, by contrast, has both an implicit balloon, the words below the image, and words depicted within the
picture.[30]

The implicit balloon contains speech of a character *heard* within that
scene; depicted words are *seen* by the character. Following Plato's *Republic*,
book 3, narratologists have made the distinction between pure narrative,
when the poet himself is speaking, and mimesis, when he gives a speech
as presented by one of his characters. Homeric mimesis could be translated into pure or simple narrative; and, conversely, the narrative can be
translated into mimesis if "one leaves out the words between the speeches

29. Kunzle, *The Early Comic Strip*, 123.
30. Larson, *The Far Side Gallery 4*, 129.

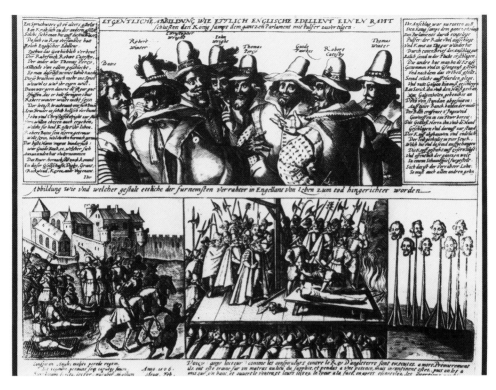

Fig. 5.   *How Various English Noblemen Decide to Destroy the King and the Whole Parliament with Gunpowder*. As published in David Kunzle, *The Early Comic Strip: Narrative Strips and Picture Stories in the European Broadsheet from c. 1450 to 1825* (Berkeley and Los Angeles: University of California Press, 1973).

and leaves the dialogue."[31] When a comic strip relies on balloons alone, as Herriman mostly does, it is mimesis, the story told only by characters speaking, without intervention of a narrator.

Words not attached to a character are, by default, narrative accompanying the picture and need not be in the present tense; as in a novel, if no individual (or group) is speaking, the words belong to that impersonal narrative.[32] When the word "CRASH!" is inserted within the picture, with-

31. Plato, *The Republic of Plato*, trans. Francis Macdonald Cornford (New York: Oxford University Press, 1945), 64.

32. See Kunzle, *The Early Comic Strip*, 132. The account by Marshall McLuhan, *Understanding Media: The Extensions of Man* (New York: McGraw-Hill, 1964), 164–69, is oddly disappointing.

out a balloon, we read it as description of the action, spoken by no one. What is crucial is that there can also be a balloon, for that makes these words *spoken* words. In Kunzle's example, *The Horrid Hellish Popish Plot* (1682), I thus distinguish between the story line below and the words spoken by the pope's agent and by a woman—"Something for a poor Scholar," "Get you gone and be hanged"—which belong individually to those two characters.[33]

With the systematic use of balloons in *Little Nemo in Slumberland* (1905–11), impersonal narrative accompanied by images is replaced by a fully integrated story using words within pictures.[34] Set in the picture in front of, or to the side of, what is represented, a balloon does not break up that space even when, in an otherwise completely dark scene, the only light is provided by the white of the balloon.[35] And yet, for the viewer—if not the depicted characters—the balloons are not transparent, for they block our view of the picture. (Sometimes in erotic cartoons the speech balloon is used to cover genitals.) We *read* the words in the balloon, but the characters in the strip *hear* them; comics translate sound and thought into images.

Any words or picture that could represent some character's thoughts may be placed in a balloon. But only occasional nonsensical images are possible, for while a character can now and then be shown thinking nonsense, a comic in which the characters had no identifiable thoughts would be like Saul Steinberg's *Comic Strip,* a representation too much like a picture of a comic strip to be a comic itself. Speech appears in normal balloons; a balloon attached with bubbles is private, known only to that character and also the viewer. Speech or thought is thus translated into visible language. Set within the picture space, the words are not elements in it; we would not see them if we could stand there in the picture; and usually the characters, who are standing there, cannot see them.

Either an element can be seen as belonging within the visual space, or it cannot. If it cannot, then it is a balloon, a container of words (or images) we read, not an object the characters could fictionally touch. No doubt this logical distinction simplifies the psychology of perception, but

33. Kunzle, *The Early Comic Strip,* 140.

34. See Meyer Schapiro, "On Some Problems in the Semiotics of Visual Art: Field and Vehicle in Image Signs," *Semiotics* 1, no. 3 (1969): 223–42.

35. Winsor McCay, *The Complete Little Nemo in Slumberland,* ed. Richard Marschall (Ardsley, Pa.: Remco Worldservice Books, 1990), 4:24.

that does not show that the distinction is unimportant. Some old masters cheat by depicting scrolls held by characters, as in Perudino's *Eternal Father with Prophets and Sibyls*, Perugia, Collegio del Cambio. Those scrolls are objects held by the prophets and sibyls, whereas a genuine balloon is not an object within the picture.[36] Lorenzo Lotto's *Lucrezia* (Fig. 6) depicts her last thoughts as words in a balloonlike inscription, but without recognizing the Latin quotation, the modern viewer is unlikely to understand this picture, which presents the balloonlike paper as a naturalistic

Fig. 6.   Lorenzo Lotto, *Lucrezia*, © National Gallery, London. Source: National Gallery.

36. John Sparrow, *Visible Words: A Study of Inscriptions in and as Books and Works of Art* (Cambridge: Cambridge University Press, 1969), 72, 78.

element in the picture space. In such old-master figurative pictures, "a written text must seem to most spectators nowadays an alien and intrusive element."[37]

Balloons are an extraordinarily useful resource for the visual artist, and so it is natural to ask why they were not employed by the old masters. Guercino's *Arcadian Shepherds* (1621–23) depicts the skull in effect speaking the words "et in Arcadia Ego." Poussin's later version of that scene contains those same words merely as an inscription, spoken by no one. But these pictures, and a few others, are isolated examples using balloon-like devices. Autonomous still lifes, landscapes, and abstractions are relatively late developments for sociological reasons. Before such genres of pictures could be made, a market for them needed to develop. Balloons could in principle be used in history painting, but inserting balloons into a Giotto or Raphael creates a very odd effect, disrupting the picture. Old masters did not need to make the story explicit by adding words. The Situationalist International's insertion of a balloon into a Delacroix (Fig. 7) was intended as a transgressive gesture. Insofar as the aim of old-master art was to tell stories without using words in the picture, such additions to the visual field are unaesthetic. Even after the invention of the comic strip, it is rare to find balloons in modernist art.[38] In Matisse's *Conversation* (1908–12) "the grillework at the window spells out 'NON.'. . . the NON becomes emblematic of the space and substance of the room, of the whole painting's thesis and antithesis of layered irony."[39] Although it is reasonable, seeing it in context, to treat this word as a thought of the woman, the effect is more subtle than setting that word in a cartoon balloon.

To reduce the comic to mere words—or, conversely, to treat it as merely a sequence of images—leaves aside what defines this art form, the integration of words with picture. According to seventeenth-century aesthetic theory, as exemplified in the paintings by Poussin, visual art is centrally concerned with the communication of emotion. In his *Judgment of Solomon* we read the contrast between the two mothers, the rightful figure, whose supplication we see, and the accusatory figure on her right, as well as the varied responses of the spectators—reflection, shock, dismay—from

37. Ibid., 48.

38. But see Pierre Couperie et al., *A History of the Comic Strip*, trans. Eileen B. Hennessy (New York: Crown, 1974), chap. 12.

39. Jack Flam, *Matisse: The Man and His Art, 1869–1918* (Ithaca: Cornell University Press, 1986), 250–52.

Fig. 7.   Yes, Marx's thought really is a critique. . . . As published in *On the Poverty of
Student Life* (Situationist International, n.d.).

their bodily gestures. In Poussin's art world it was possible to have confi-
dence in a system of universal expression. In the modernist visual culture
of the comic, such thoughts attributed to depicted figures must be spelled
out in some particular language. Unlike pictures, comics must be translated for readers who do not know their language: "zo moet Amsterdam
ook worden . . . een echte city, een zakenhart voor Europa" (that's what
Amsterdam should become—a real city, Europe's business heart").[40] For
those who cannot read Dutch, the image that accompanies these words is
unintelligible without a translation.

Words and pictures in comics are intimately connected, mutually trans-
latable, but disjoint categories of things—with but one important excep-
tion, artists' signatures and depicted words. "I've always used my signature
as line," Robert Ryman has said, "and as part of the composition"; for
him, as for many artists, signatures constitute part of the visual work with-

40. S. Davidson, *The Penguin Book of Political Comics* (Harmondsworth, Middlesex: Penguin,
1982), 190.

out being elements within the picture space.[41] The uses of words in literal ways in cubism, surrealism, and other forms of modernist art, in the astonishing works circa 1908–20 of Hilma af Klint, which use words to convey occult messages, and in Charlotte Salomon's *Theatre of Life* come after the birth of comics, which seem not to have systematically taken up such experimentation.[42]

Words in balloons represent the characters' thoughts. Where are those words in the picture space? Words in balloons are not elements within the picture; but neither are balloon words outside the picture, for they do what in old-master painting is accomplished by the characters' facial expressions; they represent thoughts inside those figures' heads. The balloon words are both inside and outside the picture in the sense that thoughts, said to be "inside one's head," do not have any position in space. (If successful materialist theories of the mind are developed, our commonsense view will be revised; but thoughts may still turn out not to have any identifiable physical location.) We cannot look inside another person's head; we can only infer that person's thoughts from their outward expression in words and gesture.

Often, as Alexander Nehamas says, "irony consists simply in letting your audience know that something is taking place inside you that they are not allowed to see—but it also leaves open the question whether you are seeing it yourself."[43] Insofar as the words the logocentric thought balloon contains are unambiguous, the balloon does not allow for such irony. If we treat the balloon contents as just dialogue accompanying the action, there is no reason these words could not just as well be presented below the picture. But adding the balloon changes the nature of a picture. In Kunzle's seventeenth-century examples, words within pictures very frequently mark the names of places and people; the words are outside the picture space. In balloons, conventional elements within the picture frame, contents of the depicted characters' minds are represented.

The discovery of perspective in fifteenth-century Florence, close-up framing devices of baroque artists, the methods for depicting water and

41. In an interview with me at his retrospective, Museum of Modern Art, New York, 27 October 1993. A portion of this interview was published as "Robert Ryman on the Origins of His Art," *Burlington Magazine* 139 (September 1997): 631–33.

42. Ake Fant, "The Case of the Artist Hilma af Klint," in *The Spiritual in Art: Abstract Painting, 1890–1985,* exhibition catalogue, by Maurice Tuchman (Los Angeles: Los Angeles County Museum of Art, 1986), 154–63.

43. Alexander Nehamas, "What Did Socrates Teach and to Whom Did He Teach It?" *Review of Metaphysics* 46 (December 1992): 297.

clouds of nineteenth-century landscape painters: many such techniques of visual representation are the product of long research. In this history the relationship between genuine discovery and mere convention is difficult to untangle. How simple, by contrast, is the speech balloon, which appears sporadically from very early on in the history of European art. The inventor of the balloon may have been Bruno di Giovanni, a friend of Buonamico di Cristofano, called Buffalmacco, a fifteenth-century Florentine artist discussed by Vasari.[44] "Because Bruno complained when he executed [a saint holding the arms of Pisa] that they were not life-like as those of Buonamico were, the latter in jest, to teach him to make figures which, if not life-like, should at least converse, made him put some words issuing from the mouth of the woman who is entreating the saint, and also the saint's reply to her. . . . This thing pleased Bruno and other foolish men of the time, just as to-day it pleases certain clumsy fellows who have thus employed vulgar devices worthy of themselves."[45] Bruno is unskilled because he is using written words to tell a story that should be communicable by visual means alone.

It is hard to know how such devices were understood before the comic strip was invented. Lacking any full contemporary commentary, it is easy to read these proto–speech balloons anachronistically. "In the medieval love of etymological thinking," Michael Camille writes, "words really were things, and if two words sounded alike it meant that what they designated must also be similar."[46] I hesitate to accept the radical historicism implicit in this account. Surely contemporary viewers of the Rohan Master's picture understood the distinction between seeing a man and reading the words on the scroll. The inscription in Luc di Tomme's *Madonna,* Millard Meiss argues, is "an active invitation to contemplate the image, to share Christ's suffering and to evaluate its quality. . . . An inscription of this kind serves precisely the same function as the saints who look appealingly at the spectator."[47] But there is an obvious difference between seeing depicted imploring saints and reading that statement.

44. Paul Barolsky, *Why Mona Lisa Smiles and Other Tales by Vasari* (University Park: Pennsylvania State University Press, 1991), 14–16.

45. Giorgio Vasari, *The Lives of the Painters, Sculptors, and Architects,* trans. A. B. Hinds (London: Everyman's Library, 1963), 1:117–18.

46. Michael Camille, *Image on the Edge: The Margins of Medieval Art* (Cambridge, Mass.: Harvard University Press, 1992), 40; see also idem, *Master of Death: The Lifeless Art of Pierre Remiet Illuminator* (New Haven: Yale University Press, 1996), chap. 6.

47. Millard Meiss, *Painting in Florence and Siena After the Black Death: The Arts, Religion, and Society in the Mid-Fourteenth Century* (New York: Harper & Row, 1973), 123.

In *Laocoon*, Lessing famously complains about the use of hieroglyphics by visual artists. When a painter uses clouds to hide his hero from the enemy, "his cloud is a hieroglyphic, a purely symbolic sign, which does not make the rescued hero invisible, but simply says to the observers,— 'You are to suppose this man to be invisible.'" It is one thing for Homer metaphorically to "depict" divine aid in the form of a cloud veiling the hero; it is quite another to use a cloud thus in a picture. Such a device "exceeds the limits of painting. . . . It is no better than the rolls of paper with sentences upon them, which issue from the mouths of personages in the old Gothic pictures."[48] As has often been noted, Clement Greenberg's canonical account of modernism offers but a variation on Lessing's theme: "Each art had to determine, through its own operations and works, the effects exclusive to itself."[49] But the rejection of Greenberg's conception of the purity of painting did not lead many artists to use balloons; such devices of comics remained alien to museum art.

Words in speech balloons function much like the interior monologue in the novel—speech in any language, real or made up, can be attributed to depicted characters. Usually one person speaks, but it is possible also to link such words to a group of speakers (Fig. 8). Such dialogue differs in kind from the narrative often found below the picture; those words, like the impersonal narrator in a novel, tell the story without taking any particular point of view. Near the start of *Sentimental Education* Flaubert uses quotation to create a shifting point of view.

> Frédéric felt a certain respect for him, and on a sudden impulse asked his name. The stranger replied all in one breath:
> 'Jacques Arnoux, proprietor of *L'Art Industriel*, Boulevard Montmartre.'[50]

In comics this effect is achieved by the balloon. The comics' dialogue must always be attributed to some character, even if, as in *Doonesbury*, that character is a politician depicted as a short-fused bomb. To parody Descartes's cogito argument, "if there is speech, there must exist a

48. Gotthold Ephraim Lessing, *Laocoon: An Essay on the Limits of Painting and Poetry*, trans. Ellen Frothingham (New York: Noonday Press, 1965), 80–81.

49. Clement Greenberg, *The Collected Essays and Criticism, Volume 4: Modernism with a Vengeance, 1957–1969*, ed. John O'Brian (Chicago: University of Chicago Press, 1993), 86.

50. Gustave Flaubert, *Sentimental Education*, trans. Robert Baldick (London: Penguin, 1964), 17.

Fig. 8.   Joe Sacco, *Palestine*, one page. © 1992. Fantagraphics Books, Inc. Joe Sacco.
Used with permission.

speaker." At the movies, seeing the characters on the screen as speaking is only an illusion—I know that these voices come from the speakers on the wall. I hear voices, but imagine them coming from the actors. If, forgetting the libretto, I read the supertitles at the opera, I *see* in English translation the words I *hear* sung in the original language without supposing that the translated words I read are being sung. When reading comics, I see the depicted words as spoken by the depicted figures. That is a different illusion—I look at words and imagine them to be spoken.

What is the nature of mental representation? The classical tradition tends to assimilate the contents of the mind to pictures, a view that already, as Hobbes noted in his critique of Descartes, raises obvious problems with ideas of beings such as God and His angels, inherently unpictorial creatures. According to classical epistemology, thought involves essentially visual representations. Some recent philosophers of mind have argued that mental representations are mostly verbal. Cartoon balloons abolish any such distinction, freely mixing words and pictures. Thoughts can be equally well represented, the comic seems to say, by words and by pictures.

In the old-master tradition, everything represented in the visual field tends to correspond to some element we could imagine touching, could we but walk into the picture space. But the speech balloon itself, though visible to us like the other depicted elements, is not normally an element in the depicted space; we can see it, but the depicted characters cannot. What in the picture space are words or thoughts in our space become representations thereof within the balloon. The balloon itself, a mere container, does not correspond to any object represented in the picture. That the thoughts or words are surrounded by a rounded shape says nothing about the nature of those thoughts or words. And yet, the specifically visual qualities of balloons also are important. Some are graceful, others chunky; insert too many balloons in the picture, and that space feels crowded. We readily compare and contrast the balloon with the depicted objects surrounding it, observing how its shape does or does not fit into the composition. The balloon thus is not just a neutral container but another element in the visual field. Indeed, even identifying balloons as containers already is to hint at some ways of identifying their expressive significance. When Jules Feiffer or Garry Trudeau suspends the words without employing such boundary shapes, the effect is subtly different.

In the manuscript illustration by the Rohan Master, *Dying Man, Struggle for His Soul, and Christ,* in which the man commits his spirit to Christ, who tells him that on judgment day he will be with Him, "[w]e cannot fail to marvel at the fact that the corpse speaks the language of the Church and of all well-educated Europeans, Latin, whereas the Deity replies in French. The use of the vernacular localizes Christ's words, and thus gives another sign of his intimate relation with the dying Frenchman. His words also award a privileged position to the French language."[51] A French painting does not need to be translated into English; a French book does. When Tintin was published in English, the word captions had to be translated. Speakers of a language, like those who have mastered any convention, find it so "natural" that reflection is needed to recall that it is a convention. It seems hard to predict what conventions are easily learned. The general rules of the theater are so familiar that it takes a little effort to defamiliarize them. In A. R. Gurney's *Sylvia*, in which a female actor in street dress and with a face mask plays a dog—a convention that takes but a moment to understand—everyone gets it.[52] With comics, what is now hard to reconstruct is how the seemingly complex conventions associated with word balloons were, without any explanation, mastered rather quickly by everyone who read them.

51. Millard Meiss, with Sharon Smith and Elizabeth Home Beatson, *French Painting in the Time of Jean de Berry: The Limbourgs and Their Contemporaries* (New York: George Braziller, 1974), 271.

52. See Marjorie Garber, *Dog Love* (New York: Simon & Schuster, 1996), 82–85.

THE IMAGE SEQUENCE; OR, MOVING MODERNIST PICTURES

Entering the Dresden Picture Gallery for the first time, I walk around the entire museum slowly, viewing the old-master paintings I know from reproductions. The relationship of these artworks to the very famous central painting in this gallery, Raphael's *Sistine Madonna*, makes this ensemble of paintings feel something like a 1980s New York–style installation. After repeated visits to such grand museums, I easily recollect the place of almost every individual painting. I can imagine walking blindfolded through the National Gallery, London, as it was arranged in the 1970s. Now, when that National Gallery has been rehung, in the new Sainsbury Wing, my experience of each individual painting, colored by what I see around it and in nearby rooms, has become subtly different. Such museums, like a comic strip, can be treated as sequences of images that thus constitute a narrative. In choosing the sequence in which art is to be viewed, the curator constructs an implicit art-historical narrative.

We can learn something about such visual narrative sequences by studying accounts of literary and visual storytelling. "[P]lot can be defined as the dynamic, sequential element in narrative literature. . . . Spatial art, which presents its materials simultaneously, or in a random order, has no plot; but a succession of similar pictures which can be arranged in a meaningful order (like Hogarth's 'Rake's Progress') begins to have a plot because it begins to have a dynamic sequential existence." Movies can then be described as "an extreme development of this plot-potential in spatial form."[1] This way of thinking treats the opposition between visual and verbal arts as essentially fixed, making it impossible to understand comics, a visual art that employs narrative sequences as fully temporally extended as those in literature.

Narrative, so everyone nowadays recognizes, is extremely important. "To raise the question of the nature of narrative," Hayden White argues, "is to invite reflection on the very nature of culture and, possibly, even on the nature of humanity itself."[2] The nature of our mental activity is represented in the structure of images and their sequences; insofar as classical philosophy of mind paid too little attention to such activities, it had an impoverished conception of our powers. Arthur Danto takes a similar view: "The principles, whatever they are, that enable us to tell and follow stories, to construct and read poetry, are the principles that bind lives into unities, that give us the sense of chapters ending and of new ones beginning."[3] My present concern is with how those principles are exemplified in the narrative structures of comics.

This second important conceptual innovation of comic strips, image sequences, is best understood in relation to narrative in traditional visual art. Comics, "a hugely narrative form," are "part of the same history occupied earlier by the bands of tableaux in the Arena Chapel in Padua."[4] They are, arguably, the natural response to the limits of traditional narrative painting. In much old-master art a text is the source of the picture, and recovering it constitutes the act of interpretation. What can be pictured can also, within limits, be said in words. We need to know the story Piero della Francesca tells in his *Legend of the True Cross* in order to understand the order of scenes and their meaning. Mystery pictures such as Giorgione's *Tempest* are very hard to interpret because no one is sure

1. Robert Scholes and Robert Kellogg, *The Nature of Narrative* (London: Oxford University Press, 1966), 207, and see also Lawrence L. Abbott, "Comic Art: Characteristics and Potentialities of a Narrative Medium," *Journal of Popular Culture* 19, no. 4 (1986): 155–76.

2. Hayden White, *The Content of the Form: Narrative Discourse and Historical Representation* (Baltimore: Johns Hopkins University Press, 1987), 1.

3. Arthur C. Danto, "Beautiful Science and the Future of Criticism," in *The Future of Literary Theory*, ed. Ralph Cohen (New York: Routledge, Chapman & Hall, 1989), 384.

4. Danto, *Narration and Knowledge*, 14.

what text, if any, is illustrated. Many genre paintings—Greuze's family melodramas, for example, based on no text—may yield, still, a narrative. In his *Salons*, Diderot readily constructs a story, turning Greuze's image into a novella. Textless pictures, Watteau's and also Manet's, anticipate the problems posed by Matisse's *Luxe, calme et volupté* (1904–5), as characterized by John Elderfield: "[N]one of [his] invented compositions . . . can be precisely matched with texts. They do not, like more traditional Western figure compositions, tell known stories. They are closer to genre than to history paintings in telling unknown stories, but they are nonetheless unlike genre paintings in that their stories are indecipherable."[5] This issue arose early in the history of European art. Was it possible that the medieval illustrator "might invent new narrative miniatures whose literary content he made up himself without relying on the written word? . . . there are definite indications that occasionally miniatures did originate from the desire of an artist to tell his own story or episode by pictorial means."[6] One way to resolve such images—that is, to interpret them—is to present a narrative about the artist, describing his personality or use of art-historical themes, as Elderfield does in offering a Lacanian narrative about Matisse's picture.

Escaping the apparent limits of visual narrative, hermetic modernist pictures threaten to be inaccessible to commentary, any paraphrase seeming to take us a great distance from the picture itself. Baudelaire sensed that modernist painting faced this problem. He described his own most advanced creative writing, the prose poems, as having "neither beginning nor end, as everything in it is both head and tail, one or the other or both at once, each way."[7] He imagined "the miracle of a poetic prose, musical though rhythmless and rhymeless," an ideal that had, he says, "its origins above all in our experience of the life of great cities." Those prose poems describe in words what the artist of modern life, that "kaleidoscope gifted with consciousness . . . reproducing the multiplicity of life and the flickering grace of all the elements of life," produces in images.[8] Baudelaire anticipates modern mass culture, art without the classical allusions of his favorite artist, Delacroix. The problem of mass-culture art is finding some

5. John Elderfield, *Henri Matisse: A Retrospective*, exhibition catalogue (New York: Museum of Modern Art, 1992), 34.

6. Pächt, *Book Illumination in the Middle Ages*, 151.

7. Charles Baudelaire, *The Poems in Prose with "La Fanfarlo,"* trans. Francis Scarfe (London: Anvil Press Poetry, 1989), 25.

8. Baudelaire, *The Painter of Modern Life*, 9

way of structuring verbal or visual representations, which threaten to become as incoherent as the modern city itself.

How can we interpret images of modern life if they do not reproduce any text to which we have independent access? In *High Art* I speak of interpretation as moving a picture, alluding to the way that, to understand an image, we must identify or construct a narrative telling what happens before and after that scene.[9] Is a suspended child being lowered, or lifted? Is the person with raised garment dressing, or undressing? As Leo Steinberg has emphasized, an image may remain ambiguous until tied to some narrative. Very often a mysterious picture would be easy to understand could we but know the previous or next moment of the action. What moment of an ongoing action should one picture show to reveal that entire action most effectively? In film the action moves automatically; in that brother art to the comic, the animated cartoon, we have the real illusion of movement. Comics and films, developing at the same time, respond to the felt need for accessible populist art. Films, obviously impressive, have deservedly received a great deal of attention from academic scholars. Comics raise different, equally interesting philosophical problems. I am unwilling to dismiss them as merely a secondhand version of movies.

To understand a picture, we must *move* the depicted scene. *Luxe, calme et volupté* and some other modernist pictures of the early twentieth century pose interpretative puzzles because they are difficult to move in this way. Taken in isolation, one panel from *Tintin in the Land of the Soviets* (1929) is difficult to understand; but set in narrative context, we readily grasp the significance of the action. Comics solve Baudelaire's problem in terms that would surprise him, creating a populist modernist art that, without appeal to any independent text, develops a lucid, easily comprehensible visual narrative. The tradition of narrative art of Piero, Poussin, and Greuze is continued by the comics artists, who, discovering a strikingly original way of telling stories with pictures, moving their images in novel ways, thus offer an alternative to the high modernism of Matisse and Picasso. Here, as in my account of balloons, I am of course not suggesting that these artists understood their achievement in this way. Only when we set their immediate concern with entertainment in this perspective is it possible to have this properly historical viewpoint on their work.

How, from discrete images, do we generate a continuous narrative? Two

9. See Carrier, *High Art*, chap. 4.

images already constitute a narrative, for their meaning is inscribed in the succession. In understanding how those pictures are connected, we imagine some appropriate action.[10] Scott McCloud's *Understanding Comics: The Invisible Art* identifies as "closure" the way that the space between panels, "the gutter," is used when the viewer "takes two separate images and transforms them into a single idea."[11] This gutter, not always a mere background, may become an active part of the image, like the frames between the images in a fresco. When, for example, we read the great *Krazy Kat* strip of 16 April 1922, a truly Matissean story about the self-referential qualities of comics, how do we bring together these successive discrete images, transforming them into one story? We construct a jumpy narrative, like a movie shown with the projector not quite in sync. Just as, when seeing a representation, we form and test some hypothesis about what is depicted, so, with comics, we construct and check a narrative that makes sense of the scenes. In Piero's Arezzo fresco *Legend of the True Cross*, it is not easy to identify the order of the scenes and to understand their significance. The story covers an extended period, and to follow it we must move from the top right down, and then back up to the top left scene (Fig. 9). Uncertainties about the possible allegorical political meaning of these scenes complicate our task. Herriman's scenes are close together, almost to the point of being successive images in a flipbook; Piero's are not, and so moving his picture requires constructing a story that includes various intermediate scenes not depicted in the picture.

McCloud asks: "Is it possible for any sequence of panels to be totally unrelated to each other?" The answer he gives is no, on the ground that no matter how dissimilar two successive images seem, "a relationship of some sort will inevitably develop."[12] Narrowly correct, his account is misleading as a general characterization of this synthesis, or what may be called closure. Occasionally a comic may use such juxtapositions, but in practice no narrative could develop unless most transitions were relatively straightforward. Pierre Couperie describes "the acceptable margin of elapsed time between two pictures . . . if they are to form a narrative continuity." Comics are like realist novels: a few odd transitions are possible only because we are accustomed to reading the body of the text as

10. Fresnault-Druelle, *La bande dessinée*, 30.

11. Scott McCloud, *Understanding Comics: The Invisible Art* (Northampton, Mass.: Kitchen Sink Press, 1993), 66.

12. Ibid., 73.

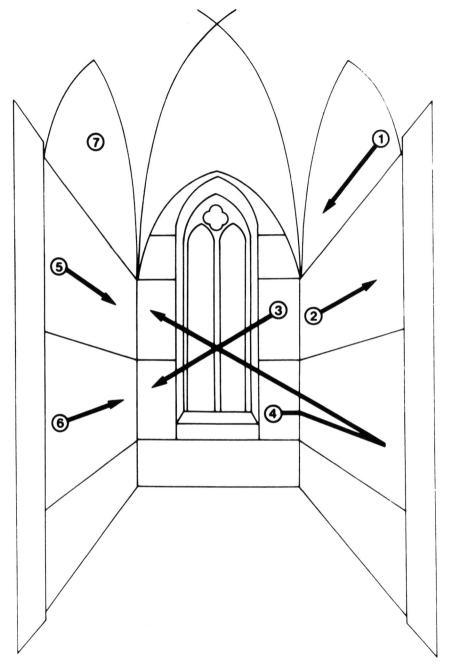

Fig. 9. Diagram of Piero della Francisca's *Legend of the True Cross*. After Marilyn
         Aronberg Lavin, *The Place of Narrative: Mural Decoration in Italian Churches,*
         431–1600 (Chicago: University of Chicago Press, 1990), diagram 34. Used
         with permission.

straightforward narrative.[13] What we often infer from transitions are causal connections. In *Tintin in the Land of the Soviets* the Bolshevik lights the fuse, and two panels later—"Boom!"—Tintin is blown up. Larson's single images imply the next moment of the action; Tintin shows two panels, asking that we connect them.

When we ask how to represent such an action, this already implies a need for depictions of before and after moments to be linked together into a continuous narrative. In Hellenistic art, Kurt Weitzmann proposes, "as the eye in reading a text moves from one writing column to another, so it moves now from one picture to the next, *reading* them, so to speak, and the beholder visualizes in his mind the changes which took place between the consecutive scenes. . . . the single scenes in a sequence contain elements which stimulate in the beholder a certain creativeness in imagining those actions which lie between the painted scenes."[14] These concerns with narrative sequence were always important. In the nineteenth century, as Jonathan Crary has shown, various optical instruments showed awareness of "temporality as an inescapable component of observation." Hence it was important to understand how "some form of blending or fusion occurred when sensations were perceived in quick succession," as when using such instruments as the phenakistiscope and the kaleidoscope.[15]

In the traditional visual narrative, as pointed out in Chapter 1, a single image is often viewed as being but one portion of an ongoing action; looking at that picture, one can reconstruct earlier and later moments of that temporally extended action. But when comics present depictions of closely linked successive scenes, their methods of narrating are closely akin to those found in novels. When, for example, in twelve images from *Dick Tracy* we view him and Lizz in pursuit of Haf-and-Haf (Fig. 10), we change point of view repeatedly, but always in ways that, with the aid of the words in balloons, permit us to see this group of pictures as stages in one continuing action, like that presented in a verbal narrative.

Much of the craft of comics involves making such transitions happen quickly enough that they do not appear static and boring, but without such large gaps as to make the action seem jumpy. Great artists make

---

13. Couperie et al., *A History of the Comic Strip*, 231.

14. Kurt Weitzmann, *Illustrations in Roll and Codex: A Study of the Origin and Method of Text Illustration* (Princeton: Princeton University Press, 1947), 17–18.

15. Jonathan Crary, *Techniques of the Observer: On Vision and Modernity in the Nineteenth Century* (Cambridge, Mass.: MIT Press, 1990), 98, 104.

Fig. 10. *Dick Tracy,* detail. As published in *Dick Tracy: America's Most Famous Detective* (Secaucus, N.J.: Carol Publishing Group, 1990). © Tribune Media Services.

their sequences look seamless. When, by contrast, the 1930s cartoonist Ed Kressy "treated each panel as an isolated illustration, some of which might be separated from their predecessors by the passage of as much as twenty or thirty minutes," the result was "that the story seem[ed] to leap-frog key moments."[16] In what is called "bad narrative breakdown" there are gaps in the story, with plot resolution "taking place 'off camera.'"[17]

Just as in reading a novel with changing viewpoints we do not need explicitly to synthesize them, imagining our implied viewing position changing, so in responding to *Dick Tracy* there is no reason to suppose that we need to calculate our place in relation to the depicted scenes. It is enough that we think of this sequence as showing rapid motion, like the scenes in many 1990s television commercials. Aware that we are look-ing from a succession of diverse vantage points, we find that change of implied position exhilarating.

Systematic use of such changing points of view is a genuine novelty in comics. Hogarth's *Rake's Progress* is not a true narrative, for the successive images present discrete events that are too distant from one another, and so require too many intermediate stages to be filled in, to be viewed as one continuous story. Neither is Piero's story of the True Cross, for what defines the image sequence in the true comic is that successive scenes are close together and in an easily read order. Reading Piero's scenes in order requires a complex movement, grasping the relationship between, say, *Dying Adam and Family* at the start and *Victory of Constantine* at the lower left demands a fairly complex reconstruction of the story. It has taken art historians some time to identify the sequence properly.[18]

Something needs to be said here, also, about the aesthetic effect of sequences of panels. As the background matters in fresco painting, so too in comics. (Frescoes need to be seen *in situ*, not just in inadequate photographic reproductions, which tend to eliminate the painted areas between individual paintings.) The background is not a neutral, merely passive element, but constitutes a distinct active visual aspect. Some com-ics display three or four panels of the same size in a horizontal array; others, *Krazy Kat*, for example, move the eye downward in what Hogarth

16. Robert C. Harvey, *The Art of the Funnies: An Aesthetic History* (Jackson: University Press of Mississippi, 1994), 15.

17. Harvey, "The Aesthetics of the Comic Strip," 648; John Canemaker, *Winsor McCay: His Life and Art* (New York: Abbeville Press, 1987), 46.

18. Marilyn Aronberg Lavin, *The Place of Narrative: Mural Decoration in Italian Churches, 431–1600* (Chicago: University of Chicago Press, 1990), chap. 4.

called the line of beauty, pleasing us by varying the size of individual panels. McCay's panels seem like separate frames of wide-screen motion-picture film, and so they anticipate his later work in animation. The viewer's point of view is like that of a movie camera pulling ahead of the action. How do these sequences constitute a narrative sequence and not just a sequence of images? What is required is the self-evident presentation of the images *as* connected, as forming a causal sequence. Difficult as it may be to specify necessary and sufficient conditions for success in this synthesis, everyone is aware of what happens when such narratives "work" or fail.

Comics occupy a fascinating place in between paintings and motion pictures. "Motion in the movies is made possible by the projector; in the comics, motion appears through our becoming, so to speak, human projectors."[19] The successive images are connected only when the reader connects them. When looking at a comic like *Tintin in the Land of the Soviets* (1929), any reader of the literature on literary narratology is likely to divide that narrative into short sequences of interlocked images broken by jump cuts.[20] Within each sequence, we understand events because the gap between successive images is relatively small. And we can follow the jump cuts because they have been motivated and are relatively infrequent. Tintin comics are structured in the same general way as Proust's novel *La recherche*. Like a novel, a comic can be arbitrarily long, but usually the central character reappears. And it may, in this way unlike most literary works, consist of a sequence of repeated episodes, the meaning of each made clear in large part by reference to the norm. (One precedent is Raymond Queneau's *Exercises in Style*, a virtuosic retelling of one story in various modes of storytelling.) *Batman* and *Superman* are extended, essentially open-ended narratives "essentially without beginning or end about a recurring set of characters on whom the reader is always dropping in *medias res*."[21] Here it is convenient to separate the short sequences from the jump cuts. Within the sequences, we willingly move backward and change our viewpoint; we are amazingly flexible, willing to keep the continuing story going. In the Tintin *Red Sea Sharks*, for example, a scene

19. Earle J. Coleman, "The Funnies, the Movies, and Aesthetics," *Journal of Popular Culture* 18 (1985): 97.

20. See Gérard Genette, *Narrative Discourse: An Essay in Method*, trans. Jane E. Lewin (Ithaca: Cornell University Press, 1980) and idem, *Narrative Discourse Revisited*, trans. Jane E. Lewin (Ithaca: Cornell University Press, 1988).

21. Inge, *Comics as Culture*, 3.

with (made-up) Arabic in the balloons fits into the narrative, and when Captain Haddock falls into bed drunk, we read without difficulty balloons with angel and devil as illustrating self-restraint and temptation.

Tintin in the Land of the Soviets, an extreme case, presents the following narrative in six scenes: Tintin is trapped in a room; he puts out the lights, and then all we see are various bubbles indicating a fight; there is one completely black square; and then with the light back on, we read him saying, "In the darkness they knocked each other out."[22] Only in the context of that sequence does the black square have meaning. In a different sequence, it might signify that the hero was knocked out or be a purely abstract image. When in *Krazy Kat* the image is dark, the balloon still is bright; not a light in the darkness, that balloon stands outside the picture space. And in Grant Morrison's visionary comic-strip novel *The Invisibles*, a totally blank white page is used to suggest a character's vision of nothingness.[23]

Because we interpret a comic by gathering together the successive scenes, it takes a certain self-conscious effort to linger on a single panel, treating it as if it were a self-sufficient picture. To understand such narratives, it is worthwhile trying some simple experiments.[24] Isolate segments, and they become highly ambiguous; those images then are more "aesthetic," like a Roy Lichtenstein painting based upon a cartoon. Remove the words in a balloon, or view the political cartoons in an unfamiliar language. Then, when that image is hard to decipher, we are puzzled, and perhaps tempted to linger. Matisse's Vence *Stations of the Cross* is as close to a cartoon as we get in modernist painting, but compared with even the most obscure Herriman, how elliptical is Matisse's narrative, winding from lower left upward, referring the eye back and forth across the entire visual field. We are accustomed to reading comics like books, moving left to right and top to bottom. It takes some effort to follow the Japanese-style samurai narrative of Takeshi Mackawa (Fig. 11), which goes from upper right, left, down the page, speech balloons in each panel running from right to left, starting at the back of the book.[25]

22. Hergé, *The Adventures of Tintin: Reporter for "Le Petit Vingtième" in the Land of the Soviets* (1929; reprint, London: Sundancer, 1989), 102–3.

23. George Herriman, *The Komplete Kat Komics* (Forestville, Calif.: Eclipse Books, 1990), vol. 6, 8 May 1921; Grant Morrison et al., *The Invisibles: Say You Want a Revolution* (New York: DC Comics, 1996), 95.

24. Experimental psychology could contribute to systematic study of these problems, which are relevant also to old-master narratives.

25. Takeshi Mackawa, *Victory for the Spirit*, trans. Jonathan Clements (London: Bloomsbury Children's Books, 1995).

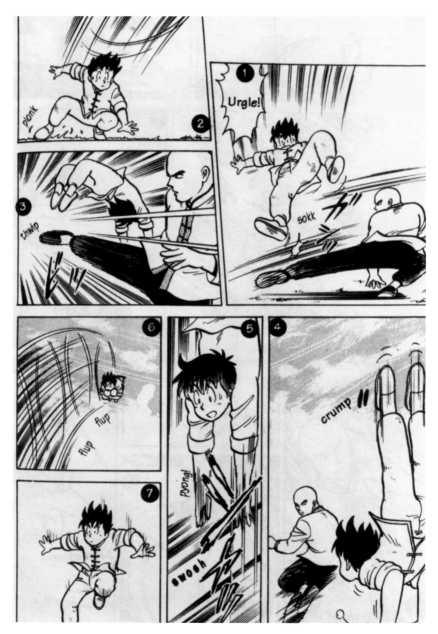

Fig. 11.   Takeshi Mackawa, *Iron Fist Chinmi, Book 4: Leap of Faith*, detail. As published in Bloomsbury Children's Books. © Takeshi Mackawa.

Granting that comics thus are a unity of images and words, how do they bind together these two elements? My answer to this question, a central one for my account, has two parts. In the next chapter I describe our experience of this peculiar word/image unity; in Chapter 5, I then indicate what kind of theory can best explain that experience.

WORDS AND PICTURES
BOUND TOGETHER;
OR, EXPERIENCING THE
UNITY OF COMICS

CHAPTER
4

I AM NOT ONLY RESIDING IN MY BODY, AS A PILOT IN HIS SHIP, BUT . . . AM
INTIMATELY CONNECTED WITH IT . . . THE MIXTURE IS SO BLENDED, AS IT
WERE, THAT SOMETHING LIKE A SINGLE WHOLE IS PRODUCED.

—DESCARTES, *MEDITATIONS ON FIRST PHILOSOPHY*

I happen to have come alone today to Mauritius, the great museum at the
Hague. As I walk through the galleries, I am interested in the response of
other viewers. My sense of Vermeer's *View of Delft* is definitely influenced
by the presence of other people, both those who know something about
art history and the naïve spectators. (When viewing visual art, even the
response of people with other goals can be revealing. Once in Arezzo,
when during mass I cautiously stepped into the back of San Francesco, I
was encouraged to walk toward the Pieros by a kindly kneeling lady who
with Pieroesque affirmative gesture waved me forward.) When then on my
return train trip to Amsterdam I turn away from the Dutch landscape to
read a novel, I am entirely caught up in my private experience, so absorbed in reading that I am startled by the friendly conductor. Talking
later to a friend about this book, which she also has read, I think of us as
sharing what were essentially private experiences.

I *read* a novel, but *see* a picture—these are essentially different forms of
aesthetic experience. When seicento theorists and modern semioticians
talk of reading paintings, they surely speak metaphorically—paintings are

not texts. It is natural in the Hague to come back repeatedly to stare at the Vermeer, comparing the painting with my recollection of reproductions. Even when looking at one isolated detail, I remain aware of the entire painting, which lies on the periphery of my vision, as when, viewing the enormous Sistine Chapel ceiling, I remain aware of the individual parts not in focus. Reading novels, by contrast, my sense of the whole artwork is inherently diffuse. I may return to favorite passages, but my attention is directed at a long text, no single page of which I can attend to entirely all at once. When I flip backward and forward in Flaubert or Proust, seeking to find a scene I recall with especial pleasure, I unavoidably reread other passages I had remembered only vaguely. While reading, it can be positively annoying to have someone looking over my shoulder. Movies, like comics, use picture sequences, but they are a social art. If I am all alone in the theater, how can I not wonder about the value of the movie I am seeing? Jacques Lacan and his commentators have presented complex theories about the relation of "the other" to the viewer.[1] My simpler point is that there is a distinction in kind between arts where other people's presence constitutes part of the viewing experience and those art forms, like comics and the novel, where it does not.

Here we return, also, to the distinction between literature, an art of time, and painting, an art of space. The experience of comics differs, in ways obviously relevant to understanding their nature, from the experience of both paintings and literature. I usually read a comic privately (like a novel), sometimes embarrassed if in the store I am seen so interested in an art form meant for children. But I "read" a visual narrative. Looking at the comics in the morning paper, I sometimes recollect the previous days' account of the lives of these fictional characters; reading these scenes is a lot like watching a television story develop from week to week while missing some episodes. New members can join the audience anytime, but "repeat viewers," who know the tale, continue to get pleasure from each episode. A movie should be viewed from the start, but in *Krazy Kat* there is no obvious overriding order to the scenes published on successive days, although they sometimes allude to contemporary politics. To begin *La recherche* around page 2000 would be perverse and surely unprofitable, but every day someone somewhere is seeing some newspaper comic for the first time. Seeing strips of *Doonesbury* or *Flash Gorden* a day at a time is

---

1. See David Carrier, "Art History in the Mirror Stage: Interpreting *Un Bar aux Folies-Bergère*," *History and Theory* 29, no. 3 (1990): 297–320.

fun, but when reading complete editions collected in books, the story soon becomes repetitive.

Nelson Goodman made famous his distinction between allographic and autographic art forms, between those arts in which "even the most exact duplication . . . does not thereby count as genuine" and those in which "the distinction between original and forgery . . . is significant."[2] His goal was to explain why a score (and a text) can be copied but a painting cannot. Comics are an autographic art with, potentially, an indefinite number of copies of the original image. In this latter sense, paintings, engravings, and comics are allographic; "initially," Goodman suggests, "perhaps . . . all arts are autographic," and the conception of allographic art develops when there comes to be a need "to transcend the limitations of time and individual," so that notated Mozart sonatas, for example, can be performed after the death of the composer.

Goodman's analysis tells how to categorize comics, but it does not explain how they are experienced or tell anything about how they differ from other visual arts. After I returned from the Hague, I found in Amsterdam a marvelous store selling "original" George Herrimans clipped from newspapers. That way of treating comics assimilates them to the Japanese woodcuts I looked at nearby in the shop of an art dealer. Herriman's images were meant to be disposed of with the newspaper; that comics usually have dates, not titles, is a reminder that they are consumed, then discarded. What constitutes, still, the lasting value of a comic like *Krazy Kat,* and thus makes it worthy of analysis, is its capacity to receive the sustained attention I have given to it. "In the visual arts," Richard Wollheim writes, "we escape, or are prised away from," what he identifies as "similarities and differences," and "are called upon to concentrate our attention upon individual bits of the world."[3] Published in 1965, in an essay with the title that seems to have named the movement, Minimal Art, Wollheim's words now inevitably carry a provocative tone; they have acquired, certainly, a political weight. When much sustained analysis is given to any individual bits of the world, be they the banal-looking artifacts of the minimalist artist or the comic strip in the newspaper, we cannot but think them of great value; individuation of precious objects goes naturally together with obsessively detailed characterization of their features.

2. Nelson Goodman, *Languages of Art: An Approach to a Theory of Symbols* (Indianapolis: Hackett, 1976), 113, 121.
   3. Richard Wollheim, "Minimal Art," in *Art and the Mind* (London: Allen Lane, 1973).

Krazy Kat modifies, in interesting ways, this well-entrenched conception of aesthetic experience. In place of the traditional focused attention on an individual visual artifact, Herriman encourages diffused awareness of an individual strip as one of many permutations on his themes. He decenters the individual image, permitting us to remain aware of the many variations on his narrative structure, which remain, for the moment, out of sight. Maybe poststructuralism has sensitized us to the special values of such art; perhaps postmodernism aids us in seeing this effect. Does earlier art anticipate this process of dissemination? Viewing one Poussin, the connoisseur brings to mind many other works by him, placing the individual object in its proper historical place. The iconographer may, in turn, look further afield, seeking sources in images by other earlier artists. The more we know about that single object's place in his development and about its visual sources, the better we will understand its unique qualities. The commentator on *Krazy Kat* is in a somewhat different situation, understanding an individual strip in part by recalling or anticipating the developments of its themes in other strips, enriching experience of what is immediately present to the eye by peripheral awareness of other related images. Unlike a Poussin, a Herriman is not a self-sufficient object. "From this absurd situation without particular comic ingredients," Umberto Eco writes, Herriman "drew an infinite series of variations, based on a structural fact that is of fundamental importance in the understanding of comics." The individual episode "acquires flavor only in the continuous and obstinate series, which unfolds, strip after strip, day by day."[4] A certain modernist artistic tradition involves working in series; in comics the play of theme and its variations is essential, for one defining quality of a good strip is that the basic story can, with minor modifications, be retold repeatedly.

Speech balloons and closely linked narrative sequences—these are the crucial, the defining, elements of comics. But there is a third way in which the comic strip differs in kind from other visual art. When earlier I compared Piero's Arezzo cycle to narratives in comics and contrasted the wordless storytelling in a Poussin to the use of speech balloons in comics' narratives, I left aside entirely questions of scale. Visual artworks, be they frescoes, panel paintings, or even old-master drawings, typically hang on walls. Spectators move around those objects. Movies, too, are public. Even when I am alone in a museum or movie theater, I am aware that others

---

4. Umberto Eco, "On 'Krazy Kat' and 'Peanuts,'" *New York Review* 32, no. 10 (1985): 25–27.

may enter this public space. By contrast, I read alone, without needing company or desiring that another person look over my shoulder. (Families who read aloud together create a kind of home theater.) Comics are read like books, by one person, who by turning the pages determines how fast he or she moves through the narrative.

The frames of old-master paintings function as a visual complement to the image. When, by contrast, many large modernist works are left un-framed, that procedure says something about the informality associated with this art. "Without a frame, the painting appears more completely and modestly the artist's work."[5] With the comic strip, the edge of the page functions like a frame. Comics, however, differ from both old-master and modernist paintings. In their admixture of image and word, comics are an in-between art—in scale, and so also in the relation they establish between viewer and object. Drawings may be as small as comics, but when framed and hung on museum walls, we respond to them as if they were paintings. When I framed the Herrimans I purchased in Amsterdam, I treated them like the old-master prints I occasionally collect, and so viewed them similarly. Seeing them in my study, I give these comics more sustained everyday attention than the strips in the Pittsburgh newspaper, which I only glance at over breakfast.

Much is to be learned about comics by reflection upon the differences between the modes of attention demanded by this art form and those associated with painting and literature. Kant is concerned, Michael Podro notes, to explain what it means to say that "our experience is unified," considering "what powers of the mind must be posited in order to produce such unity"; "unity or order are not something that . . . could be provided by the material presented to the mind, but only something the mind itself imparts."[6] The difficulty, Podro goes on to observe, is then to understand how it is possible to have any experience that is not in some nontrivial sense unified. Looking at my messy desk as I write this sentence, I see a heap of books, photocopies, and plates, all relevant to the finished book you are reading. These materials are waiting to be synthesized for this writing project. The unity of what to an intruder might seem a rather chaotic assemblage of objects is defined by the structure of my intentions as they are spelled out in this manuscript. Everything on the desk has its proper place in this text.

5. Schapiro, "On Some Problems in the Semiotics of Visual Art," 228.
6. Michael Podro, *The Manifold in Perception: Theories of Art from Kant to Hildebrand* (Oxford: Clarendon Press, 1972), 13.

Different problems about unity arise with painting. Heinrich Wölfflin's discussion of the different forms of unity in classical and baroque art contrasts sixteenth-century art, where "the separate elements of the organism, conditioning each other and holding each other in harmony, take effect," and seventeenth-century paintings, with that "absolute unity in which the individual part has lost its individual rights."[7] Inspired in part by the Kantian formalist tradition, Wölfflin's goal was to describe the various ways in which pictures can be unified. An image has many identifiably distinct parts, so how can we both observe those individual elements and think of them as inextricably bound into one organic whole? Paintings are traditionally praised for their organic unity—for gathering a multitude of separate elements, so that no essential part is either superfluous or omitted, into one perfectly unified whole.[8] Apart from monochromatic paintings, all pictures have many discrete parts—and even an apparently homogeneous monochrome has top and bottom, and left and right, sections.

Sydney J. Freedberg's beautiful formalist descriptions recount how, for example, in Giorgione's *Castelfranco Madonna*, the artist "has connected parts he may have described precisely into an arbitrary smoothed pattern to make a purified and artificial whole."[9] His book, which I took along in the car trunk when I drove to view that picture, provides an account that seems true to my experience. But the danger, Gombrich has observed, is that such mere appeals to unity fail to provide genuine explanations.[10] Good pictures are unified, and bad ones not. Who can doubt that? But what remains difficult is verbalizing that important distinction in convincing, noncircular ways. Art historians, accustomed to think of stylistic questions in empirical terms, are unlikely to find much aid in philosophers' abstract ways of talking about unity. Almost everything we see has parts, and so appeals to general conceptions of our synthesizing mental powers seem unlikely to teach much about what concerns the historian, the achieved unity, or relative disunity, of individual pictures. Wölfflin's

7. Heinrich Wölfflin, *Principles of Art History: The Problem of the Development of Style in Later Art*, trans. M. D. Hottinger (New York: Dover, n.d.), 156–57. See the commentary in Michael Podro, *The Critical Historians of Art* (New Haven: Yale University Press, 1982), chap. 7.

8. See the discussion, with bibliography, in Richard Wollheim, *Art and Its Objects*, 2d ed. (Cambridge: Cambridge University Press, 1980), sec. 59.

9. S. J. Freedberg, *Painting in Italy, 1500 to 1600* (Harmondsworth, Middlesex: Penguin, 1971), 79.

10. See E. H. Gombrich, "Raphael's *Madonna Della Sedia*," in *Norm and Form: Studies in the Art of the Renaissance* (London: Phaidon, 1966).

(and Freedberg's) practice suggests that art-historical judgments of unity tend to be comparative. It may be hard to characterize in so many words Piero's unities, but comparing them with Giotto's and Michelangelo's is suggestive; and contrasting all of these pictures to Chinese landscapes can help to identify their shared "Italian" unities.

Visual artworks employing both words and images raise different questions about unity. In Bible illustrations made around 1100, Otto Pächt writes, "an inner contact between picture and script is never established, and the picture remains a cumbersome alien body in the book."[11] What by contrast the ideal comic should provide is precisely such a contact between image and word, to the point that the two form an ideal unity. "An inscription may be thought to be an alien and intrusive element in a picture"—intrusive because words and images differ in kind—and so it is natural to ask which, in any given comic, is more prominent.[12] "The subordination of the pictorial to the literary," Lawrence Abbott writes, "is one of the subtlest realities of the medium."[13] Logically speaking, there need be no reason that the coexistence of words and pictures in a unified comic should cause problems. Just as a landscape painting can contain buildings, human figures, and landscape harmoniously set together without need for a hierarchy, so a comic book can bring together both words and pictures. But here, as with any binary opposition, it is natural to ask which element is more important. In comics, will words dominate pictures, or do words subordinate themselves to the visual component?

Comics closely integrate words and pictures. Are they textual narratives with illustrations or, rather, pictures accompanied by texts? An argument for the former view might appeal to the fact that the comics can be paraphrased in words, as if they were novellas. So, for example, *Batman and Robin*, "What a Sweet Racket" (1 November 1943 to 7 January 1994), is the story of a missing convict who abducts Robin, fails to capture Batman, and is caught when Batman realizes that his own escape implicates a private detective who was secretly working with the mob.[14] But such a paraphrase leaves out what is distinctive about this comic, the interplay

---

11. Pächt, *Book Illumination in the Middle Ages*, 129.

12. Sparrow, *Visible Words*, 88.

13. Abbott, "Comic Art," 156.

14. *Batman Dailies: Volume I*, 12–46; further references are incorporated directly into the text. On plots and literary interpretation, see Alexander Nehamas, "Mythology: The Theory of Plot," in *Essays in Aesthetics: Perspectives on the Work of Monroe C. Beardsley* (Philadelphia: Temple University Press, 1983), 180–96.

of image and text. So, for example, in the introduction to this story we have description of the spotlight that "flashes a giant cone of light—etching an eerie symbol against the sky!" (14)—and the bat-shape (Fig. 12); and the action frequently depends upon visual devices, as when we read in a balloon the detective's hidden response to Batman's praise of his cleverness, "Cleverer than you think, **Batman!**" (35). Paraphrasing a painting in words would leave out its visual elements, and (to some significant degree) the same is true with this comic.

"We still tend to look at illuminated manuscripts with eyes too much conditioned by wall and panel painting to interpret them correctly."[15] The only way of doing justice to any art form is to find its own proper descriptive terms. That comics combine these two different devices is one source of the feeling that they are an awkward in-between art, neither purely literary nor just entirely visual. Looking at comics, it is often said, is neither proper reading nor genuine viewing; too much attention to comics is thought to be bad for children, for it keeps them from learning how to do genuine reading. "Two separate techniques must be employed

Fig. 12.   *Batman*, 28 October 1943, detail. As published in *Batman Dailies, Volume I: 1943–1944* (Princeton, Wis.: Kitchen Sink Press, 1990). © Kitchen Sink Press.

15. Pächt, *Book Illumination in the Middle Ages*, 9.

by youngsters; two separate literacies."[16] How appropriate that this in-between art form was invented by Rodolphe Töpffer, a would-be painter who turned to writing and caricature because of problems with his eyes. What identifies the comic book for many commentators is its deficiency, its failure to be either a real text or just a proper image.

In *Seduction of the Innocent*, Fredric Wertham's famous moralizing critique of 1950s comics, the author complained about these in-between artworks: "Comic-book readers are handicapped in vocabulary building because in comics all the emphasis is on the visual image and not on the proper word."[17] He is unwilling to think of reading comics as a special skill, different from, but not necessarily therefore lesser than, book reading. Gombrich has made this point in a more neutral way: "What I find very interesting is that so many half literate or illiterate can read the comics because they are combined with images. This combination is apparently much easier than either only images or only texts."[18] Sometimes the felt problem with these combinations of images and words is that comics readers fail to learn to read properly. Comics undo knowledge of real reading: "those with good reading ability . . . are *seduced* by comic books into 'picture reading'" (my italics). Not surprisingly, Wertham objects also to another kind of what might be called inbetweenness encouraged, so he thinks, by comics—homosexuality. Looking critically at his claims, which had great practical effect on the comics industry, how striking is his reliance upon anecdotal information, without the pretense, even, of statistical argumentation: "It is true," he writes, "that many children read comic books and few become delinquent. But that proves nothing. Innumerable poor people never commit a crime and yet poverty is one of the causes of crime."[19]

In 1946, Robert Warshaw complained that "the comic strip has no beginning and no end, only an eternal middle. . . . This . . . is a characteristic of Lumpen culture: all gradations and distinctions are broken down, even the distinction between art and life."[20] Comics, as he described them, anticipate the painting of Robert Rauschenberg and Andy Warhol

16. Ronald Schmitt, "Deconstructive Comics," *Journal of Popular Culture* 25 (1992): 157.

17. Fredric Wertham, *Seduction of the Innocent* (New York: Rinehart, 1954), 125. See Mark West et al., "Dr. Fredric Wertham," *Comics Journal* 123 (December 1989): 76–87.

18. A portion of this interview was published as "The Big Picture: David Carrier Talks with Sir Ernst Gombrich," *Artforum*, February 1996, 66–69, 106, 109.

19. Wertham, *Seduction of the Innocent*, 139, 245.

20. Robert Warshaw, *The Immediate Experience: Movies, Comics, Theatre, and Other Aspects of Popular Culture* (Garden City, N.Y.: Doubleday, 1962), 53.

and much of what has been commonly identified as postmodernist art.
More recently, writing in a similar vein, Robert Hughes has worried about
how "the rapid negligence of Warhol's images parodied the way mass
media replace the act of reading with that of scanning."[21] Like Warshaw,
he is concerned about what happens when the scanning of sequences of
pictures replaces traditional reading.

No doubt Warshaw was correct to object to the nasty content of many
of the comics of his day—the examples he cites are alarming; and Hughes
certainly is right to have problems with mass-media images. But since
such rebarbative content can also be found in much traditional literature
and visual art, what is interesting about their complaints is the focus on
how what might be called the formal structure of such images is threaten-
ing. Breaking down seemingly essential boundaries is often thought to be
unnatural, and so morally pernicious, as is shown by the moralizing discussed critically in Tim Clark's social history of Impressionism:

> The boundaries between moral laxity and prostitution seemed to be
> dissolving, and this was held to be the more dangerous because it
> was not just sexuality that strayed over into the public realm, but
> money—money in fleshy form.
>
>   The environs of Paris . . . were neither town nor country any
> more.[22]

Women, whores or wives, whose role was hard to identify; parts of the
city that were hard to place: they were felt to be dangerously disorienting.
The once famous Villa Borghese *Hermaphrodite*, now in the Louvre, was
said to cause visitors "to blush with pleasure and shame simultaneously."[23]
One Lady called it "'the only happy couple she ever saw.'" Even those
lucky people, gay or straight, who can enjoy being attracted to someone
of the "wrong" sex are, I suspect, likely to find that experience mildly
disconcerting. We expect the world to fit our preconceived stable categories, and so what falls in between is easily felt, depending upon our tem-

21. Robert Hughes, "The Rise of Andy Warhol," in *The First Anthology: Thirty Years of "The
New York Review of Books,"* ed. R. Silvers, B. Epstein, and R. Hederman (New York: New York
Review of Books, 1993), 221.

22. T. J. Clark, *The Painting of Modern Life: Paris in the Art of Manet and His Followers* (New
York: Alfred A. Knopf, 1984), 107–8, 151.

23. Francis Haskell and Nicholas Penny, *Taste and the Antique: The Lure of Classical Sculpture,
1500–1900* (New Haven: Yale University Press, 1982), 235.

perament and politics, to be either exciting or menacing. Hence the fascination with, and fear of, cross-dressing, androgyny, people of "mixed-race," comics, and other forms of in-betweenness.

A comic strip uses text and picture to tell one story—and so it is unified insofar as every element, visual and verbal, contributes to that end. Rationally speaking, why should there be any potential conflict between words and pictures when they work together to achieve that single end? A painting has many parts; a novel, many words; a comic, many images *and* words: we synthesize that multiplicity of elements to experience the artwork's unity. But we are not entirely rational, and so readily find something troubling about combinations of different arts. Roger Fry's perplexed description of what he believed was the inevitable lack of unity of opera displays this view: "[I]n so far as one was really interested in the drama, one began to be impatient at the slowness of the music, which, of course, was absurd, seeing that the only really important esthetic event was, so evidently, the music itself. . . . perfect co-operation between two arts becomes difficult in proportion as they reach a high pitch of intensity or completeness of expression."[24] And the stage sets further divide our attention. Fry does not have any conception that drama, music, and sets could be working together to create one unified experience of the total artwork; for him, seeing an opera is like listening to a pianist while simultaneously a juggler performs nearby in front of a painting. The juggler and the painting would inevitably distract the audience from the pianist.

In what Rensselaer Lee calls "the humanistic theory of painting," the goal was that of oratory, which "had been concerned not merely with words, but equally with gesture and facial expression as vital means of conveying human emotion."[25] "As is poetry, so is painting"—according to the classical accounts these sister arts have similar goals, which they achieve in essentially different ways, painting displaying in a single image what poetry can reveal only in a narrative.[26] If we take this tradition seriously, there is reason to expect conflicts in combinations of words and images. Insofar as such an artwork is visual, how could its all-at-onceness as picture be readily combined with its verbal narrative qualities? These classical ways of thinking, which do not do justice to modernist art, ex-

24. Roger Fry, *Transformations: Critical and Speculative Essays on Art* (Garden City, N.Y.: Doubleday, 1956), 37, 45.
25. Rensselaer W. Lee, *Ut Pictura Poesis: The Humanistic Theory of Painting* (New York: W. W. Norton, 1967), 9, 25.
26. See Lee, *Ut Pictura Poesis*.

press still well-entrenched critical clichés that heavily influence how comics have been understood.

Once we acknowledge that all experience of art—whether reading literature or seeing pictures—involves synthesizing separate elements, why should comics and opera, which involve more than one kind of element, pose any special problem? If verbal and visual arts differ in kind, then they demand different, essentially opposed forms of attention. To look at a shape, viewing it formally, and to read a word involve essentially different, perhaps inevitably incompatible forms of attention. It is possible to evaluate a word aesthetically without knowing anything of the language. Fry admired Chinese paintings, enjoying "the graph of a dance executed by the hand."[27] We all experience such defamiliarization when visiting an unfamiliar culture. Something may be learned about our own culture by learning how it is seen by an outsider. "I walk the London streets," a Chinese author writes, "without any sensation of surprise at the shopsigns or advertisements in the windows, for they are almost all stylistically identical. They are neat, regular and symmetrical, but they are collections of lifeless letters."[28] In China, by contrast, the corresponding advertisements are "an attraction to people of taste," who are calligraphy lovers. When in the European Middle Ages "objective representation [was] transformed into abstract ornament and reconverted into the former," words treated like images, a similar process occurred.[29]

If experience of words as words differs in kind from the experience of images as images, then how can images and the words in balloons and below the images ever constitute a genuine unity? A philosopher may here be tempted to draw an analogy with Descartes's account of the unity of mind and body. Persons are unities of bodies and souls, things of distinctly different sorts that traditionally are given radically different value. Body and soul are linked in two ways: in action the soul moves the body; in sense perception, modifications of the body affect the soul. When I decide to act, I voluntarily move my limbs; when aroused erotically by what I see, imagine, or feel, my body is affected directly. In such situations my immediate experience seems to be undivided; only philosophical reflection suggests that the self might be composed of the two distinct substances Descartes identifies. The unity in comics of image and text is,

27. Fry, *Transformations*, 97.

28. Chiang Yee, *Chinese Calligraphy: An Introduction to Its Aesthetic and Technique* (Cambridge, Mass.: Harvard University Press, 1973), 4.

29. Pächt, *Book Illumination in the Middle Ages*, 57.

ideally, as close a bond as this unity of body and soul bound together to form a person.

I mean this comparison of comics and persons as something more than an analogy. Comics, with their balloons, represent that relation of inner states and outward bodily expression which characterizes persons. Comics mimic in their narrative sequences that process which, if classical philosophy of mind is correct, characterizes perception. From a sequence of discrete individual sense impressions, philosophers have argued, we construct our world. Comics are personlike in their unity of words and images because they depict fictional persons whose actions are represented. Philosophical theories of the mind-body problem aim to explain that unity or to dissolve it. Comics merely illustrate this dualism, without taking any stand on philosophical questions about the nature of the mind-body relationship. In his account of Saul Steinberg, an artist who stands apart from, and yet is so close to, comics, Danto, speaking in terms familiar from his book on Sartre, notes that philosophers have "distinguished between the view we have of the world insofar as we are subjects of consciousness, and the view of us others have who perceive us as objects—between life as it is lived from the inside, as it were, and life lived in the recognition that we have an outside as well."[30] The word balloon, by externalizing thoughts, makes visible the (fictional!) inner world of represented figures, externalizing their inner lives, making them transparent to readers.

Narrative sequence is for Danto a second feature of central importance in the structure of consciousness. He makes an analogy between this knowledge of other minds and what he calls "historical consciousness," which also "sees events as having an inside and an outside." To be historically conscious (in this broad sense) is to be aware of the immediate present as one of a sequence of moments, to "perceive both it and one's consciousness of it as something the meaning of which will only be given in the future."[31] In externalizing this awareness, displaying the antecedents and consequences of one moment, comic-strip narratives thus show what it is to be a person. A cognitive psychologist who invented a working version of the ring of Gyges—permitting us to look into the minds of others and see their inner thoughts—would but duplicate the balloons in

30. Arthur C. Danto, *Saul Steinberg: The Discovery of America* (New York: Alfred A. Knopf, 1992), vi.

31. Danto, *Narration and Knowledge*, 343, 342.

comics. Reading these narratives is to look into the minds of the fictional characters, as if their inner worlds had become transparent to us.

The assumption shared by those who like and those who dislike comics is that they are a mixed art form, part word and part image. The problem of the medieval illustrator, Pächt writes, was "reconciling the requirements of pictorial space with that of the painted surface of the page of the book."[32] Comics, it might seem, should be understood similarly. A product of mass culture, they use popularized versions of images from traditional visual art, supplemented with words to serve as easily accessible narratives for semiliterate audiences. Movies serve that same public, but they are a genuinely novel invention, the product of truly original technology; comics, by comparison, are inherently a compromise visual art form.

My analysis, reinforced by the analogy of comics with persons, argues for a different, radically opposed view. Comics permit us to see, in retrospect, what was the essence of painting (the essence of European painting; Chinese art has quite different concerns). They show how the needs of narrative painting naturally led to the employment of speech balloons and visual sequences. Comics thus make explicit the problem implicit in narrative painting: How is it possible to tell a story without reference to some prior text? For classical figures like Poussin, narration often requires appeal to prior knowledge of the story. The tradition I described in Chapter 3—the art of Hogarth, Greuze, Manet, and Matisse—involves the systematic development of visual narratives that do not rely upon prior knowledge of the story. Far from being an odd or marginal form of visual art, comics are of central importance because they thus mark the natural limits of this mainline modernist tradition. I reject the claim that because comics use both images and words, they are essentially a jury-rigged art. What defines narrative in the comic strip is that picture and text work together to tell *one* story. Once we focus on the nature of comics as narrative, we will cease to be tempted to think that their unity is any less natural than that of paintings or novels.

Having identified the three essential qualities of comics—the speech balloon, the closely linked narrative, and the book-size scale—now it is time to discuss the interpretation of this art form. That is the task of the next chapter.

---

32. Pächt, *Book Illumination in the Middle Ages,* 77.

PART TWO

INTERPRETING COMICS

THE CONTENT OF THE FORM; OR, SEEING PICTURES, READING TEXTS, VIEWING COMICS

CHAPTER 5

THE ONLY STATES OF AWARENESS WHICH I CAN REGARD AS "POSSIBLY MINE," IN THE SENSE THAT I COULD HAVE THEM AND KNOW THAT I HAD THEM, ARE ONES WHICH INCLUDE AN AWARENESS OF MYSELF, AN ABILITY TO HAVE THE THOUGHT THAT *THIS IS HOW IT IS WITH ME NOW.*

—JONATHAN BENNETT, *KANT'S ANALYTIC*

Traveling on Italian trains in the 1970s, I often saw adults reading comic-strip versions of novels, picture books like those I had read as a child. In Italy full mass literacy was a relatively late development. Looking forward to the paintings and sculptures I had come a long distance to look at, often reading fiction to pass the time, I never reflected on the relation of these comics to the old-master Italian visual art of interest to me. Only more recently have I come to recognize that the connections between comics and paintings deserve discussion. Any novel can be turned into a comic—a story told in words might also be presented in words and pictures. But in practice the formal structure of the comic strip seems heavily to influence its content. Kunzle's seventeenth-century struggles between Jesuits and Protestants are not so different in kind from those of the modern morality plays in which Superman, Batman, and Little Orphan Annie struggle against evil in its many forms. Visual narrative sequences using balloons seem to have a natural affinity with these themes.

A spectator becomes absorbed in a painting; a reader gets engrossed in a text. Although a great deal of concern in art history and literary theory is devoted to characterizing these modes of attention, less has been said about how to compare our experience of these art forms; that no doubt is a natural omission, given that they are thought to be so different. "Speaking for myself," Roger Fry says of Daumier's *Gare St. Lazare*, "the first impression . . . is of the imposing effect of the square supports of the facade, the striking and complicated silhouette of the man to the right, the salience of the centre figure so firmly planted on his feet. . . . The first effect, then, is mainly of feelings aroused by plastic relations."[1] Only after a page of such formalist analysis does he add: "[A]ll this time we have been entirely forgetting plastic and spatial values we have, through vision, plunged into that spaceless, moral world which belongs characteristically to the novel, and we can hardly help noticing, by the way, how distinct this state of mind is from that with which we began." If we accept the traditional contrast between the visual arts of space and literary arts of time, then thus to identify the storytelling elements of a painting is surely to be distracted from its properly visual formal aspects.

Other formalist art historians have described looking at pictures in different ways. For Jean-Baptiste Greuze, Michael Fried writes, "it is as though the presence of the beholder threatened to distract the dramatis personae from all involvement in ordinary states and activities, and as though the artist was therefore called upon to neutralize the beholder's presence by taking whatever measure proved necessary to absorb, or reabsorb, those personae in the world of the painting." Diderot believed that painting "depended upon the supreme fiction that the beholder did not exist, that he was not really there, standing before the canvas."[2] Fried draws analogies between paintings, especially paintings explicitly involved with storytelling, and the theater. Just as actors can pretend that the audience is not present, so the painter's depicted figures can be shown as if they, were they actually actors, would not notice the viewer's presence. He contrasts this absorptive imagery to theatrical art, which, incomplete in itself, exists only in relation to some spectator.

How little relation these two different accounts of painting have to our experience of comics. Fry's productive fiction—his idea that we can sepa-

---

1. Fry, *Transformations*, 20–21. The painting he describes is apparently lost. For a recent social history of this (and related Daumiers), see Bruce Laughton, *Honoré Daumier* (New Haven: Yale University Press, 1996), chap. 7.

2. Michael Fried, *Absorption and Theatricality: Painting and Beholder in the Age of Diderot* (Berkeley and Los Angeles: University of California Press, 1980), 68, 103; on Fried, see Carrier, *Artwriting*, chap. 3.

rate entirely our response to formal and literary elements—is hardly possible to take seriously in dealing with an art form in which visual and verbal aspects are so intimately intermingled. For Fry, comics combine two essentially different arts—literature and painting. Fried's immensely suggestive idea that sometimes we can treat the depicted figures as if they were unaware of our presence is a possible view of persons represented in paintings. But it is hardly a reasonable way of responding to the tiny figures depicted in a comic. The figures depicted in comic strips are like the imagined people presented in novels; when reading Flaubert or Proust, I am hardly tempted to suppose that their characters can observe or overhear me.

More can be learned about how to describe our experience of comics by considering theories of reading. "Every sentence contains a preview of the next and forms a kind of viewfinder for what is to come," Wolfgang Iser writes; the connections established in this reading process "are the product of the reader's mind working on the raw material of the text, though they are not the text itself—for this consists just of sentences, statements, information, etc."[3] Just as, according to classical epistemology, the knower constructs the world from the scattered experiences of sense perception, so the printed text is the material from which the reader creates the literary work. The same can be said about pictures. "Perception is an active matter and involves construction," Nelson Goodman says, "in that you have to read pictures. . . . you build your percepts, scanning a picture . . . and actively reconstructing it."[4] The differences between synthesizing pictures and synthesizing texts are perhaps matters of degree. Because we cannot see all of a text at once, it is natural that theories of reading consider the ways in which we construct a narrative from the printed words we see.

"To read," Roland Barthes claims in a deservedly influential analysis, "in fact, is a labor of language. To read is to find meanings, and to find meanings is to name them; but these named meanings are swept toward other names: I name, I unname, I rename: so the text passes: it is a nomination in the course of becoming, a tireless approximation, a metonymic

---

3. Wolfgang Iser, "The Reading Process: A Phenomenological Approach," in *Reader-Response Criticism: From Formalism to Post-Structuralism*, ed. Jane P. Tompkins (Baltimore: Johns Hopkins University Press, 1980), 54.

4. Quoted in David W. Ecker and Stanley S. Madeka, *Pioneers in Perception: A Study of Aesthetic Perception* (St. Louis, Mo.: Cemrel, 1979), 160.

labor."[5] Other commentators argue with aspects of Iser's and Barthes's accounts, but what for my present purposes is most suggestive is their obviously plausible idea that the text is a construction of the reader, a product of our attending to the printed words. We the readers, in synthesizing the successive scenes, recalling earlier events, and anticipating the conclusion, create the literary artwork from those mere printed words, which are but ink on the page. (This analysis might be pressed one step further. What is a printed word but a sequence of letters, marks requiring identification *as* a word to be read?) Viewing a painting is an active process; but typically the entire artwork stands at some distance from us, unlike a book, which we read held in our hands. Even if no one else is in the gallery, painting is a public art; literature, by contrast, involves private experience.

In interpreting a puzzling old-master work, the modern historian dealing with a distant culture must reconstruct the artist's intentions as best as possible for someone coming from another perspective. Speaking of "the re-creative experience of a work of art," Erwin Panofsky contrasts the naïve viewer with the art historian who "*knows* that his cultural equipment . . . would not be in harmony with that of people in another land and of a different period."[6] Panofsky's target is the connoisseur. Unmediated perception of such a painting, he is arguing, cannot reveal its intended significance. Interpretation of some of Nicolas Poussin's paintings is difficult because there are serious uncertainties about how to re-create his culture. Jasper Johns is, more or less, of the same "land and period" as his interpreters, but commentary on his deliberately hermeneutic art faces the same problem. We need to engage in the interpretative act of re-creation because we cannot know the meaning of an artwork simply by looking at it. To understand an image, we must know something of the artist's intentions—we need to re-create the artist's goals and purposes.

This very influential humanistic way of thinking has recently been attacked by commentators who appeal to Michel Foucault's "What Is an Author?" and Roland Barthes's "Death of an Author." When we properly historicize "the author," Foucault argues, we recognize that this figure, a relatively recent creation, is even now in the process of disappearing.

5. Roland Barthes, *S/Z*, trans. Richard Miller (New York: Hill & Wang, 1974), 11.
6. Erwin Panofsky, *Meaning in the Visual Arts: Papers in and on Art History* (Garden City, N.Y.: Doubleday Anchor, 1955), 18, 19.

[T]he "author-function" is tied to the legal and institutional systems that circumscribe, determine, and articulate the realm of discourses; it does not operate in a uniform manner in all discourses, at all times, and in any given culture; it is not defined by the spontaneous attribution of a text to its creator, but through a series of precise and complex procedures; it does not refer, purely and simply, to an actual individual insofar as it simultaneously gives rise to a variety of egos and to a series of subjective positions that individuals of any class may come to occupy.[7]

Thus the "author-function" of Caravaggio is to define the unity of an oeuvre whose interpretation is governed by highly speculative reconstruction, from surprisingly thin nonvisual evidence, of that man's personality, in ways that perhaps reveal as much about the ideals of the culture and writer performing the act of interpretation as about Caravaggio himself.[8] To assume that we can reconstruct the "author-function" of Caravaggio simply by looking at his art is an assumption that both Panofsky and Foucault would reject. This activity of reconstruction, as Panofsky acknowledged, is inevitably circular, our image of Caravaggio suggesting how to understand his paintings and vice versa.

Such appeals to the author, Foucault argues, necessarily are reductive: "The *explanation* of a work is always sought in the man or woman who produced it, as if it were always in the end, through the more or less transparent allegory of the fiction, the voice of a single person, the *author* 'confiding' in us." To "give up" the author is to recognize that attempts to decipher a text are futile. In truth, "a text is made of multiple writings, drawn from many cultures and entering into mutual relations of dialogue, parody, contestation," and we best understand how they are held together by appeal to the reader or, in visual art, to the viewer.[9] The man we call Caravaggio developed his artistic style by means of a complex dialogue within the very rich inheritance of Italian painting.[10]

The recent biographies of Foucault and Barthes show one obvious con-

7. Michel Foucault, *Language, Counter-Memory, Practice: Selected Essays and Interviews*, ed. Donald F. Bouchard (Ithaca: Cornell University Press, 1977), 130–31; see also Alexander Nehamas, "Writer, Text, Work, Author," in *Literature and the Question of Philosophy*, ed. Anthony J. Cascardi (Baltimore: Johns Hopkins University Press, 1987), 267–91.

8. See Carrier, *Principles of Art History Writing*, chap. 3.

9. Foucault, *Language, Counter-Memory, Practice*, 143, 148.

10. See Roberto Longhi, *Caravaggio* (Rome: Editiori Riuniti, 1968).

ceptual flaw in this argumentation.[11] Learning of Foucault's personal en-
joyment of sadomasochism does, in my opinion, surely help explain the
obviously fascinated discussion of the judicial murder of a parricide in
Discipline and Punish, a book I greatly admire; knowing about Barthes's
obsessively meticulous ordering of his desk, set up exactly the same way
in Paris and his country house, aids in explaining his attraction to structuralism. Interpretation employs all possibly useful information. It would
be unreasonable to exclude such facts about these authors' lives from analysis of their texts. While there is no reason that information about the
author should occupy a privileged role in interpretation, there is, equally
well, no warrant for its exclusion.

And yet, for my present purposes, much is to be learned from Foucault's
and Barthes's displacement of the focus of attention from the artist to the
audience, for their procedure is very useful for understanding comics. The
comic strip, as much as old-master painting, involves self-expression. It is
easy to connect what is known of Harold Gray's life to *Little Orphan
Annie*, or Hal Foster's personality to *Tarzan*. Learning that Chester Gould,
fascinated by police work, was inspired by Sherlock Holmes, why should
one not use that information when reading *Dick Tracy*? The ways a historian can use the life of a comics artist to understand his art does not differ
in kind from the way a biographer of Michelangelo can use that artist's
life to explain his art. The defining quality of popular culture comes in
how we use such information—the difference between museum art and
comics is less a fact about how the work is produced than a difference in
our attitude toward its interpretation. Learning that Winsor McCay had
a stressful marriage and George Herriman a seemingly happy one certainly
explains some differences between *Little Nemo in Slumberland* and *Krazy
Kat*. But this information really is not especially relevant to explaining
how the public responded to these comics.[12] Indeed, the way in which
comics are made shows the relative unimportance of the individual artist.
Very often famous painters have studio assistants, and so there always is
legitimate concern about the extent to which a painting has been executed by the master him- or herself. Comics sometimes are team products,
and often, after its creator retires (or dies), a strip is continued by another
artist, who works in the style of the original, modernizing its subjects. No

11. I make this conceptual point without judging the accuracy of James Miller, *The Passion of
Michel Foucault* (New York: Anchor Books, 1993), and Louis-Jean Calvet, *Roland Barthes: A
Biography*, trans. Sarah Wykes (Bloomington: Indiana University Press, 1995).

12. See Canemaker, *Winsor McCay*.

one could keep doing Picassos after his death; but *Superman* continues to appear after the death of his creator.

That "Herriman was a Negro posing as a white . . . would explain the two significant themes—illusion and rebellion-submission."[13] But even if his racial background helps explain why Herriman focused on those themes, it says nothing obvious about why his comic attracted so many people. Why did images showing "illusion and rebellion-submission" fascinate many people? "It is sadly ironic," bell hooks rightly observes, "that the contemporary discourse which talks the most about heterogeneity, the decentered subject, declaring breakthroughs that allow recognition of Otherness, still directs its critical voice primarily to a specialized audience that shares a common language rooted in the very master narratives it claims to challenge."[14] Commentators on comics can avoid this problem by recognizing that since we the audience project into a comic our fantasies, fears, and hopes, analysis needs to explain what attracts us to a successful comic—its image of our shared desires, presented in ways we can adapt for our individual purposes.[15] We don't need bookish analysis to understand such pictures, which rely only on ideas known to everyone in our culture.

Batman, telling of pure good defeating evil, presents a story anyone can immediately understand. Perhaps Batman and Robin can be viewed as a crypto-gay couple, as Wertham feared and some recent commentators hope. But what boys or girls—even those who are hopelessly heterosexual—couldn't recognize themselves in these heroes, who are so much stronger and faster than they are? And who wouldn't want to do good, as they do, aiding the poor and helpless? The great blues singers—Ray Charles, Sam Cooke, Otis Redding, and Joe Tex—have a large audience because almost everyone experiences the blues. Comics are similar. Whether or not athletic, what kid wouldn't desire Superman's ability to fly and lift heavy objects? However you judge his politics, can't you, like me, admire Steve Canyon's cool under pressure? Not that I think these characters admirable in every way: I can enjoy watching Dirty Harry shoot

13. Arthur Asa Berger, *The Comic-Stripped American: What Dick Tracy, Blondie, Daddy Warbucks, and Charlie Brown Tell Us About Ourselves* (Baltimore: Penguin, 1973), 69.

14. bell hooks, *Yearning: Race, Gender, and Cultural Politics* (Boston: South End Press, 1990), 25.

15. A fuller account of these issues would need to examine the role of rhetoric; see the brief remarks in Danto, *The Transfiguration of the Commonplace*, and Alexander Nehamas, "Pity and Fear in *The Rhetoric* and *The Poetics*," in *Aristotle's Rhetoric: Philosophical Essays*, ed. David J. Furley and Alexander Nehamas (Princeton: Princeton University Press, 1994).

thugs without reading them their rights, but upon mature reflection, I would not approve of his actions.

Popeye, Li'l Abner, and Tarzan are much odder sorts of heroes, harder to identify with and harder to describe adequately. "Popeye's figures are, to the thoughtful, symbols of a nostalgia for the free, conscienceless exercise of force. *Superman* . . . has been much criticized for this. . . . But Popeye was saved from all such pessimistic exegesis by his total unreality."[16] This discussion seems to me overly intellectual—it is like wondering if eating spinach really makes you strong. I enjoy Popeye in the way that I like my more eccentric friends. Not role models, such people are amusing because they are unusual. As Al Capp rightly noted about his characters, "I imagine most of us feel just like the Yokums now and then, don't we?"[17] I have fun reading adventures of fictional characters with whom I can identify only in limited ways—admiring their persistence and determination while aware that my life is different from theirs. What is interesting to the aesthetician is what happens when such art goes too far. *Little Orphan Annie*'s politics certainly are obtrusive, and the racism of many older comics makes them impossible to enjoy today. Like many older and some very recent *New Yorker* cartoons, these images are too nasty to please me. At a certain point, the demands of morality intervene, and I avert my eyes with displeasure.

Much humor walks this thin line between pleasurable play with transgression and presentation of frankly unacceptable materials; Oscar Wilde's audiences, like Liberace's, took aesthetic pleasure in talk about behavior that, if acted out in a more literal way, they would have found genuinely shocking. This is one reason why it is interesting and essential to learn how women and minorities respond to popular culture. Comics tell something about the social role even of those who have until recently had a relatively marginal place as creators and intended consumers of this art. Contemporary comics tell us about ourselves; comic strips from earlier times are tools for the social historian. A detailed book relating a long-running comic like Tintin to contemporary politics could be very revealing.[18]

The interpretation of comics (and other genuine mass-culture art) thus differs in kind from analysis of museum paintings. Art historians bring

16. Stephen Becker, *Comic Art in America* (New York: Simon & Schuster, 1959), 90–91.

17. Capp, *Li'l Abner Dailies, Volume One*, 5.

18. See Benoit Peeters, *Tintin and the World of Hergé,* trans. Michael Farr (London: Methuen, 1989).

close what is distant, reconstructing the intended significance of images containing depictions of enigmatic actions. In comics, word balloons and narrative sequence present the story transparently, making the meaning of the depicted action obvious to everyone in the culture. Given the limits of our knowledge, there is room for legitimate disagreement about the meaning of many old-master pictures. But almost everyone understands a commonplace comic strip without any need for explanation. You don't need to know anything, apart from that shared knowledge we all possess about contemporary everyday life, to interpret comics.

Poussin's *Landscape with Orion*, telling the story of Orion, temporarily blinded for his attempted rape of Diana, presents a legend intriguing to the scholar who reconstructs this now bookish picture, fascinating in part because its worldview has become so alien.[19] We cannot understand frankly esoteric paintings by Poussin or Jasper Johns by merely looking. But everyone knows enough to read comics. What we learn from these mirrors of our culture are some things about ourselves. The reception of Poussin reveals the tastes of a small seventeenth-century French and Italian elite; the fascination with Johns tells of the tastes of the present-day minority who take gallery and museum art seriously. But the audience for such paintings always has been very limited. The response to populist art forms reveals a great deal about widely shared beliefs. A successful comic strip must engage the fantasy life of many different people, which is why interpreting that work tells us a great deal about ourselves. As Champfleury recognized, "popular imagery, in pleasing the people, reveals their nature."[20]

Everyone is accustomed to treating popular movies as showing our shared ways of thinking and our cultural ideals. One new film, we say, fails to resolve its emotional conflicts, thus showing that no one knows how to deal with the American economy; another treats women neurotically, thus demonstrating, we suggest, the limits of the seeming success of feminism. Films thus provide a shared social framework for discussion—they let us talk about our common culture. Contemporary movies fascinate because they are "signs of the times"—and older movies are mirrors revealing shared ways of thinking from our past. There thus is a difference in kind between museum-based high art, supported financially by an elite

---

19. William Hazlitt, attuned to such themes, was able to intuit the picture's theme; most modern observers find the picture hard to understand. See David Carrier, "Blindness and the Representation of Desire in Poussin's Paintings," *res* 19/20 (1990/91): 31–52.

20. Champfleury, *Son regard et celui de Baudelaire* (Paris: Hermann, 1990), 216.

and popularized in mass media and in undergraduate art history classes, and genuinely popular art, which everyone understands and can purchase. In April 1952 Dick Tracy appeared in 507 newspapers, with an estimated readership of 80 million daily, 110 million on Sunday.[21] No museum art has ever commanded such an audience. Before a painting by Piero I ask myself, is Professor Marilyn Lavin's account right? Only scholars like her can interpret such artifacts with authority. Before a Larson, I am usually certain that I, like everyone who reads the newspaper, am "getting it." Cartoon strips are self-interpreting pictures. The narrative sequence, by moving the initial picture, dictates an interpretation. In reflecting on comics, we reverse the usual direction of interpretation. To find that image's meaning, we look not to the life of its creator but to the public response.

What then are the philosophical implications of this practice of comics interpretation? That is the topic of the next chapter.

---

21. Garyn G. Roberts, *Dick Tracy and American Culture: Morality and Mythology, Text and Context* (Jefferson, N.C.: McFarland, 1993), 288.

INTERPRETING A
POPULIST ART FORM;
OR, THE LIBERATING FORCE
OF *KRAZY KAT*

CHAPTER **6**

"DE-SEVERING" AMOUNTS TO MAKING THE FARNESS VANISH—THAT IS,
MAKING THE REMOTENESS OF SOMETHING DISAPPEAR, BRINGING IT
CLOSE. DASEIN IS ESSENTIALLY DE-SEVERENCE.

—HEIDEGGER, *BEING AND TIME*

When young I was fascinated by comic books. Long before I knew much
about museums or anything about art history, my parents made for me a
Superman cape. And like most adolescents, I eventually turned away to
more serious reading, coming back to comics only when sometime in the
1970s I purchased David Kunzle's great survey, *The Early Comic Strip*.
What then seemed desperately depressing to me about most of the morality plays he surveys, scenes of Jesuits murdering Protestants or Christians
persecuting Jews, was what I also recalled from my childhood reading—
the tedium of endless, never-to-be-resolved stories of absolute good strug-
gling with evil in its many guises. The obvious limits of Superman mark
the limits of this genre of art. Even now, in the 1990s, although Superman
has long hair and Lois Lane a more assertive role, the basic story line
remains unchanged; how indeed is it possible to tell a genuinely interesting story about an all but invulnerable hero?[1] This is why my favorite

1. The central argument of this chapter derives from Alexander Nehamas, "Serious Watching," in *The Interpretive Turn: Philosophy, Science, Culture*, ed. David R. Hiley, James F. Bohman,
and Richard Shusterman (Ithaca: Cornell University Press, 1991), 260–81. Some essays in Hor-

comic is Herriman's *Krazy Kat*. One aim of this chapter is to explain why I admire *Krazy Kat* so much.

"No sooner is an image presented as art than, by this very act, a new frame of reference is created which it cannot escape. It becomes part of an institution as surely as does the toy in the nursery."[2] To understand comics, we need to analyze the institutional framework within which they are seen. They are read so casually that often their highly original features are taken for granted. A famous inaccessible painting readily inspires curiosity; comics, read over breakfast, seem to be "just there." Travel to a distant city on another continent naturally inspires attention to visual experience, for at first everything looks strange. At home, we tend too easily to take the interesting oddities of our own urban landscape for granted. Comics, similarly, are close at hand, and so can be tricky to interpret.

What is far away must be brought close for us to see it properly. Interpretation brings close what originally was far away, explaining what appears mysterious, describing strange-seeming things in ways that make them understandable by relating them to what we know intimately. When an artist's world is temporally distant or unfamiliar, then interpretation of his work requires grasping uncustomary ways of thinking. A living artist, too, may create distance between himself and his audience. Understanding what is right at hand is an inherently different process. A number of philosophers have characterized this activity. The later writing of Wittgenstein assembles an array of banal examples, materials so familiar from everyday experience that we may not comprehend their significance, failing to realize, as his follower Norman Malcolm says in a great phrase, nothing is hidden. Heidegger, speaking of "that kind of concern which manipulates things and puts them to use[—]and this has its own kind of 'knowledge'"—talks about the "readiness-to-hand" of equipment.[3] "Dasein brings things close," a commentator argues, "in the sense of bringing them within the range of its concern, so that they can be experienced as

---

ace Newcomb, ed., *Television: The Critical View*, 5th ed. (New York: Oxford University Press, 1994), a reference I owe to Nehamas, support my claims. On Superman, see Neil Harris, "Who Owns Our Myths? Heroism and Copyright in an Age of Mass Culture," in *Cultural Excursions: Marketing Appetites and Cultural Tastes in Modern America* (Chicago: University of Chicago Press, 1990), chap. 11.

2. Gombrich, *Meditations on a Hobby Horse*, 11

3. Heidegger, *Being and Time*, 95; see also Donald Davidson, *Inquiries into Truth and Interpretation* (Oxford: Clarendon Press, 1984).

near to or remote from a particular Dasein."[4] When we move from sight to touch, from what is far away to what we are immediately in touch with, we know things differently. Walter Benjamin's much discussed account of the modern destruction of the aura, "the unique phenomenon of a distance, however close" a historical object may be, shows how movies, like comics, are a response to this "urge . . . to get hold of an object at very close range by way of . . . its reproduction"—or, more exactly, by way of this art that usually exists only in the form of reproductions.[5]

When Roland Barthes investigates how bourgeois culture "transforms history into nature," his seemingly different concerns also are relevant here. In interpretation of what is right at hand, we make explicit what, until thus articulated, is merely implicit. Looking in a critical way at the everyday ideologies of our culture, viewing that culture as if from outside, our ordinary life-world then appears transfigured. These interpretative concerns are characteristic of present-day culture and art. In the modernist tradition, Richard Shiff writes, "the indexical function has been privileged over the iconic." For us "a mark refers to its maker (or cause) more emphatically than it refers to some detached object which may happen to exhibit formal qualities consistent with the configuration of one or more marks."[6]

All of these descriptions of understanding what is close at hand are relevant to comics. Leo Steinberg describes "the tilt of the picture plane from vertical to horizontal as expressive of the most radical shift in the subject matter of art, the shift from nature to culture."[7] Turning away from high art to comics, images so close at hand as to seem unremarkable, and so be almost unnoticeable, an analogous movement takes place. I regard this as a very radical shift in interpretation, for it reverses the direction of analysis.[8] Now, instead of looking toward the distant world of the artist

---

4. Hubert L. Dreyfus, *Being-in-the-World: A Commentary on Heidegger's "Being and Time,"* *Division I* (Cambridge, Mass.: MIT Press, 1991), 130–31.

5. Walter Benjamin, "The Work of Art in the Age of Mechanical Reproduction," in *Illuminations,* trans. Harry Zohn (New York: Schocken, 1969), 222, 223; see also David Carrier, "Le opere d'arte false nell'era della riproduzione meccanica," in *Museu dei Musei,* exhibition catalogue (Florence: Littauer & Littauer, 1988), 29–34.

6. Richard Shiff, "Cézanne's Physicality: The Politics of Touch," in *The Language of Art History,* ed. S. Kemal and I. Gaskell (Cambridge: Cambridge University Press, 1991), 139.

7. Leo Steinberg, *Other Criteria: Confrontations with Twentieth-Century Art* (New York: Oxford University Press, 1972), 84.

8. On cultural studies and American art criticism, see David Carrier, "Memory and Oblivion in Contemporary American Art: The Lesson of *Artforum,*" in the proceedings of the Twenty-Ninth International Conference on the History of Art, Amsterdam, 1996 (forthcoming).

and his culture, we rather look to ourselves, understanding images by analyzing our response to them.

"To deny the large camp component of Batman is to blind oneself to one of the richest parts of his history," Andy Medhust says. "And if I want Batman to be gay," he adds, "then, for me, he is."[9] I agree entirely. Herriman's work, similarly, is what we his readers want it to be, for it is about all of us, his audience, whatever kind of individuals we may be. Treating old-master art in this subjective way is inherently problematic. When Rudolf Arnheim read my account in which I identify myself with Nicolas Poussin in his *Self-Portrait,* he rightly remarked on the oddity of my taking such an attitude toward a frigidly distant seventeenth-century painter.[10] Knowing that the painting was made using a mirror, I inferred that Poussin had to be standing in front of that mirror. But imagining, then, that I am the artist, however logical a purely geometric analysis, is a problematic interpretation, for Poussin sets himself far apart from the viewer. But in sympathetically reading Herriman's comics, we become like his characters, pursuing a slightly absurd, engrossing, endless, utterly pleasurable activity. It is appropriate to identify with his characters.

Are comics an art of social protest, or do they encourage conformity? There is a long tradition of leftist and anarchist uses of this populist medium, as in Jean Lagarrigue's story of the disappearance of the Statue of Liberty (Fig. 13); but the art itself can of course be used for other political goals or employed apolitically. What political views you read into many comics depends in large part upon your own politics. Here, as has been said of Tintin, "you love a book, in general, because of what you recover in it of what you dream of being."[11] The great American comics artists, practical sorts of people in a highly commercial business, quickly became very successful, most of them financially. Comics must be readily accessible to a mass audience; destined to be read quickly, they are, unlike old-master artworks, not usually contemplated at length. But this does not show that comics are simpler than old-master paintings. A proper theory

9. Andy Medhurst, "Batman, Deviance, and Camp," in *The Many Lives of the Batman: Critical Approaches to a Superhero and His Media,* ed. Roberta E. Pearson and William Uricchio (New York: Routledge, Chapman & Hall, 1991), 149–63; T. S. Eliot said something like this about *The Waste Land,* telling "one inquirer that the real meaning of the poem is that which it holds for whoever is reading it" (Peter Ackroyd, *T. S. Eliot: A Life* [New York: Simon & Schuster, 1984], 309).

10. See David Carrier, "Poussin's Cartesian Meditations: Self and Other in the Self-Portraits of Poussin and Matisse," *Source* 15, no. 3 (1996): 28–35.

11. Pol Vandromme, *Le monde de Tintin* (Paris: La Table Ronde, 1959), 128.

Fig. 13.   Jean Lagarrigue, *Les Aventures de Miss Liberty*, detail. © Jean Lagarrigue.

should explain how the great popular artists were able to engage the attention of a wide public. The wonderful account of Krazy Kat by George Seldes gives a clear, plausible, and affectionate explanation of his popularity: "The strange, unnerving, distorted trees, the language inhuman, unanimal, the events so logical, so wild, are all magic carpets and faery foam—all charged with unreality. Through them wanders Krazy, the most tender and the most foolish of creatures, a gentle monster of our new mythology."[12] This good text is much simpler than Marilyn Lavin's twenty-seven-page discussion, with full footnotes, of Piero's Arezzo fresco, an artwork that has fewer panels than one month's production of *Krazy Kat*.

Comics are about their audience, we readers who project into them our desires. That claim is compatible, still, with critically evaluating accounts of this popular art form. Compared with art historians' accounts, most interpretation of comics is rudimentary, lacking in detail, unsubtle in its claims, undemanding in its conceptual terms. Cartoons tend, as yet, to be discussed in too simple ways: "Krazy is not only a cat but a *black* cat. . . . At the time Krazy began to appear . . . the black cat was enjoying an unprecedented notoriety . . . the symbol of workers' sabotage, or 'striking on the job.'"[13] Compared to Lavin's intricate discussion of the political interpretations of Piero's work in Arezzo, which involves complex debate with other well-developed discussions, this is an unnuanced account. More evidence than is cited would be needed to convince me that this is the "meaning" of Krazy's blackness. "The essential triangle and repeated action," Adam Gopnik writes, "is more or less what would have happened had the Fall never taken place, and Adam and Eve . . . been left alone in Eden forever." If, that is, Adam and Eve were "a single being, the sexually ambivalent Krazy," then Ignatz would be the serpent and Offissa Pupp the Archangel Michael.[14] But this is just mistaken—there is evil, Ignatz's brick throwing, recognized as such by Offissa Pupp. Thomas Inge writes: "[U]nderlying the action is a deep-rooted sense of determinism and Naturalistic despair."[15] Is this correct? What instead strikes me is how Herriman's strip revels in obsessive repetition, which the characters (and so

12. Gilbert Seldes, "The Krazy Kat That Walks by Himself," in *The Seven Lively Arts* (New York: A. S. Barnes, 1957), 217.

13. Rosemont, "Surrealism in the Comics I: Krazy Kat," 125.

14. Adam Gopnik, "The Genius of George Herriman," *New York Review of Books* 33 (December 1986): 19.

15. Inge, *Comics as Culture*, 52.

also the reader who would find pleasure in such a narrative) enjoy. How unhappy Krazy becomes when occasionally he fails to be beaned on schedule by Ignatz!

Much straightforward information about comics has as yet not been used by commentators. What should we make of the story about Herriman's view of Kat's gender, as told to the Hollywood director Frank Capra: "I fooled around with it once; began to think the Kat is a girl—even drew up some strips with her being pregnant. It wasn't the Kat any more. . . . Then I realized Krazy was something like a sprite, an elf. They have no sex."[16] When given literary or sociological interpretations of his strip, "Herriman is supposed to have once responded . . . with the astonished reply that he merely drew a comic about a cat and mouse."[17] But until relatively recently, before art historians turned to look in close detail at Piero's works, commentary on him was no more developed.[18] Giorgio Vasari devotes only about one page to Piero's Arezzo cycle, which is within walking distance of his home. He seemingly says very little about what so productively preoccupies Lavin: the narrative sequence, the place of this work in the fresco tradition, and the symbolism possible in such works. Vasari's text is unillustrated; Lavin presents twenty-seven photographs, some illustrations of details, comparison images, and one diagram in her analysis. What encourages focus on details is the availability of such photographs and the now well-developed literature, which readily provokes further argumentation. Although *Krazy Kat,* the subject of many books, is the most famous comic, there has been little art-historical discussion of Herriman's visual sources, stylistic development. There is no critical mass of literature on this comic.

Comparing and contrasting such inherently different visual art forms as comics and old-master paintings without hidden bias is tricky. Just as no individual square on the chessboard has a privileged place, for each place has its value in the game only in relation to all the others, so in a structure containing Joan Miró and George Herriman their work has equal value because each of them occupies an equally important place in the structure.[19] Rejecting Heinrich Wölfflin's version of structuralism, his sty-

16. Quoted in Patrick McDonnell, Karen O'Connell, and Georgia Riley de Havenon, *Krazy Kat: The Comic Art of George Herriman* (New York: Abrams, 1986), 54. See also Inge, *Comics as Culture,* 46.

17. Havenon, *Krazy Kat,* 111.

18. See Carrier, *Principles of Art History Writing,* chap. 2.

19. This idea I owe to Arthur C. Danto, "The Artworld," *Journal of Philosophy* 61 (October 1964): 571–84.

listic comparison of the classical and baroque, Gombrich argues that this way of dealing with art's history is inherently fallacious because it is ahistorical.[20] Although Caravaggio chose to paint otherwise than his precursor, he could not have chosen to paint otherwise than his successor.

The most distinguished discussion of the relationship of comic strips to high art is the brilliantly useful book by Kirk Varnedoe and Adam Gopnik accompanying *High and Low: Popular Culture and Modern Art,* the much criticized 1990 Museum of Modern Art show. My present analysis builds upon some criticism of theirs. Rejecting the claim that George Herriman was not a surrealist, on the plausible ground that his "style was fully evolved before Surrealism existed," they seek "a real visual parallel that unites *Krazy Kat* and European Surrealism." In a number of Miró's paintings of the mid-1920s, they argue, "there is positive affinity with Herriman's comic strip." But identifying such affinities, they worry, "wrench[es] imagery out of its social context and create[s] false resemblances based only on superficial matches between essentially different art-making activities."[21] Miró borrowed from Herriman, but not vice versa; and so here too, do we not ultimately judge in terms of what Gombrich calls a hidden norm?

Their analysis, they seem to be worrying, will be critically dismissed, as was William Rubin's formalist 1985 show *Primitivism and Modern Art.* Rubin assembled a sequence of comparisons, as in a slide show, without asking their meaning. Varnedoe and Gopnik argue that Marxist materialists, as well as those who believe in "genius," must explain such parallels. But the real problem has nothing to do with the analysis they offer of these visual similarities. Consider how they compare essentially different art forms. Taking one of Herriman's images out of the context of its original sequence and comparing it with a Miró painting omits Herriman's words, ignores any difference in scale between the works, and leaves aside the role of Herriman's visual narrative, in which that image tells a story. In comics, as Charles M. Schulz notes, the unit of discourse is the sequence: "It is difficult to judge the quality of a comic strip in the manner that one would judge a painting because a comic strip does not stand as a single work of creation."[22] Varnedoe and Gopnik fail to take seriously the essential qualities of comics.

20. See David Carrier, "Art History," in *Contemporary Critical Terms in Art History,* ed. R. Nelson and R. Shiff (Chicago: University of Chicago Press, 1996), 129–41.
21. Varnedoe and Gopnik, *High and Low,* 172–73, 175.
22. Quoted in Berger, *The Comic-Stripped American,* xi.

Varnedoe and Gopnik explain how popular images influenced painting, as when Warhol and Lichtenstein appropriated these images to make paintings. That is a completely legitimate art-historical concern, but for all of their sympathetic fascination with comics, the result inevitably is to marginalize them, treating them as a source for museum art.[23] Gopnik and Varnedoe criticize Clement Greenberg's account of kitsch, which now shows its period style, for making a rigid opposition between serious high art and less demanding popular works. The result, they correctly observe, is to treat high art/low art connections as one-way relationships, low art borrowing from high, without considering also the ways in which high art takes from popular media. But their view of popular culture has the same problem as they identify in Greenberg's discussion. Varnedoe and Gopnik look seriously at comics, but only ultimately to subordinate them to paintings. The very format of their exhibition undercuts their capacity for independent analysis. Willing to take comics more seriously, valuing them for themselves, I want to understand their intrinsic qualities. Their influence on high art is quite another issue.

When moving from paintings to comics, a different sort of looking is called for—not the concentration of aesthetic seeing but the movement through a rambling narrative sequence. In this way, comics are more like novels than visual artworks. What remains difficult is characterizing our experience of comics in a nonreductive way. Showing that Herriman anticipated Miró doesn't demonstrate that Herriman was a serious visual artist; this comparison merely shows that the standards of painting are the wrong ones by which to judge comics. A nonreductive evaluation of the comic strip requires identifying its essence, and so understanding in a positive way how it differs from other visual and verbal art forms. The standards of comics include inventiveness, originality, and consistency. The best comics really are great artworks—great by the intrinsic standards of that art form.

Batman and Superman can struggle endlessly, for they are as immortal as their ultimate foe, evil. Individual criminals die or are imprisoned, but crime continues. With *Superman,* as commentators have remarked, the obvious difficulty is motivating conflicts when, after all, almost nothing on this planet and no one can harm him (hence the value of occasional

23. When Varnedoe and Gopnik reproduce, not Herriman's work as it appeared in newspapers, but original ink drawings, some owned by an important collector, they signal this natural bias. The permanent display of the Museum of Modern Art contains paintings by Warhol and Lichtenstein, but not, as yet, strips by George Herriman.

introductions of Kryptonite), a difficulty reminiscent of the traditional Christian dilemma about the existence of evil. How different is *Krazy Kat!* Ignatz gets a brick; he throws it and hits Kat; Krazy is pleased, but Offissa Pupp sees the action and is not; and so Ignatz ends up in jail. A cat ruled by a mouse who likes punishment; a dog on the cat's side. These unnatural relations take place in a site exotic enough to look unnatural to one European commentator, Umberto Eco, though in fact it is one of Herriman's favorite places, Monument Valley, Arizona.

Because the basic narrative structure of *Krazy Kat* is so obvious, you don't need to know all the episodes to make sense of any individual one. Herriman's amazing virtuosity, which can be fully appreciated only by reading a long sequence of these strips, consists in providing almost endless variations on this basic theme and introducing amusing subplots. He is the one comics artist I can read more or less forever without ever, even for a moment, being bored. Herriman continues the drama underwater with a struggle between Kat-Fish and Mannie Mush Rat; in a role reversal has Offissa Pupp imagine throwing the brick and then jailing himself; and even, at least once, has Krazy Kat bean Ignatz.[24] There is a Katbird who takes Krazy flying;[25] and Ignatz's wife and children come into the story when he, after stealing from them money for a brick, jails himself to escape their wrath. There are episodes centered on other characters, like Joe Stork and the brickyard owner; and there is much playful self-conscious concern with the nature of representation.

In this narrative without development, Krazy Kat wants to be hit, and is; Ignatz doesn't want to go to jail, but cannot escape. Unlike *Tintin, Superman,* or *Batman,* this strip does not show a struggle between good and evil, starkly opposed, but repetitive play.[26] In those moralizing comics, there is no conclusion because evil can never be defeated. Good must struggle endlessly against equally persistent evils. The story goes on forever, for what could count as resolution? Tintin is not the sort of person to give up or accept defeat, but his struggles feel exhausting. Were I Tintin, I would retire to my country house and disconnect the phone. Krazy and his companions also battle endlessly, but they enjoy their conflicts. So do

---

24. Havenon, *Krazy Kat,* 114, 118, 123.

25. George Herriman, *The Komplete Kat Komics* (Forestville, Calif.: Eclipse Books, 1991), vol. 7, 10 September 1922.

26. See Dennis Dooley and Gary Engle, *Superman at Fifty! The Persistence of a Legend* (Cleveland: Oxtavia Press, 1987) and Thomas Andrae, "From Menace to Messiah: The Prehistory of Superman in Science Fiction Literature," *Discourse* 2 (summer 1980): 84–111.

I, for their disputes are, happily, too petty to be moralized about. In *Krazy Kat* sublimated struggle is pleasurable. No doubt the basis of the story, Krazy's pleasure in pain, is perverse, but what strikes me most on rereading is Herriman's characters' shrewd, sensible management of conflicts. The comic might thus be called "desire and its discontents."[27] Herriman's strip can be read as demonstrating either the nasty aggression that lies right underneath the surface peace of Arcadia or, as I prefer (but this probably is a matter of temperament), the happy harmony that results from sublimating aggression. Anyone of any race, gay or straight, who enjoys family life, or would like to, will, I suspect, find Herriman's world irresistible.

Like any Arcadia, Coconino County, identified in the incomplete annotated edition, lies outside history and "civilization," apart from the public events mentioned in passing. Krazy Kat is infantile or (is this perhaps the same thing ultimately?) posthistorical. Whatever happens in this narrative is preordained—nothing new can happen. History is not over so much as not yet started. Herriman is conservative or, if you will, utopian. Matisse imagined the moment of studio work set outside time, the paradise he found, so he wrote, when he worked; Herriman discovered a similar situation. Matisse's triangular structure, artist/model/representation of model, deserves comparison with Herriman's three actors. Matisse's pictures, I have argued, "are situated *as if* in the immediate present of the spectator. . . . [They] give us the illusion of seeing the making of the very pictures we are perceiving."[28] In the 1920s the two artists shared a fascination with the self-reflexive aspects of art making. Matisse's various self-portraits with model create the illusion that we the viewers are caught in the immediate present moment of that act of picture making. The idea that it was possible to escape from history into the studio is only a fantasy; still, it may on occasion seem a good fantasy. In his great strip for 16 April 1922 (Fig. 14) Herriman sought the same infinite regress. "The story I am telling," he seems to say, "is only an illusion. Still, it is a pleasurable illusion." Knowing ourselves to be caught in history, we may find Coconino County immensely desirable, for it promises escape from all conflicts. Does *Krazy Kat* then seem, as William Empson says of another arcadian artwork, *Alice in Wonderland*, complacent? Perhaps, but I myself would prefer to stress its affinities with aesthetic detachment. Paintings generate

---

27. There is, as Alain Rey nicely says, reserved for Krazy "the indecipherable zone of desire" (*Les spectres de la bande: Essai sur la b.d.* [Paris: Éditions de Minuit, 1978], 97).

28. Carrier, *Principles of Art History Writing*, 229–30.

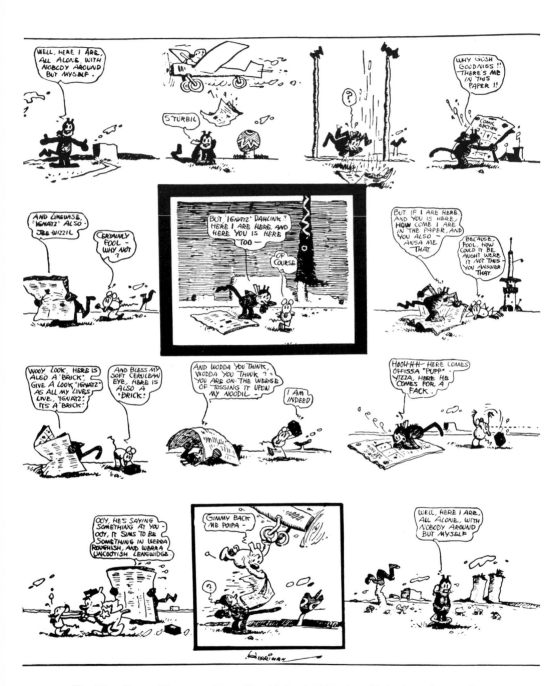

Fig. 14.   George Herriman, *Krazy Kat*, 16 April 1922. As published in *The Komplete Kat Komics: Volume Seven—1922* (Forestville, Calif.: Eclipse Books, 1991). © King Features.

this aesthetic dimension of experience by holding the eye, settling the viewer before one fixed scene; most comics, by contrast, rush forward, but in *Krazy Kat* that movement is balanced by this obvious felt lack of motion, by stasis that is but another name for visual bliss.

"As successive generations view an object of art," Shiff claims, "it acquires layers of interpretation. A knowledge of such interpretation . . . normally precedes any actual experience of viewing."[29] Paintings become hard to see without awareness of the interpretative clichés, which theorize visual artworks. How then do we view visual art before it comes to possess such a history of interpretation? In 1924 Seldes wrote: "Krazy Kat . . . is, to me, the most amusing and fantastic and satisfactory work of art produced in America to-day."[30] When everyone in their large audience "gets" comics, what is there for an interpreter to explain?[31] As everyone knows, Herriman's story has four stages: Ignatz gets a brick; he throws it and hits Krazy Kat; Krazy loves being beaned, but Offissa Pupp sees the action; and so Ignatz ends up in jail. No character ever learns anything from experience. A large ambiguously gendered cat who likes punishment, controlled by a small brick-throwing male mouse; a dog on the cat's side: this group of characters, who generate the basic narrative, have entirely illogical relationships, but once we accept them, the rich array of *Krazy Kat* stories are possible. Thus, in the 11 January 1920 strip Ignatz flees Krazy, mistaking him for Offissa Pupp (Fig. 15); in the 25 January strip, Krazy proposes marriage to Ignatz, who answers with the usual brick; and on 1 February, Krazy, behind a wall with a row of other cats, is found by Ignatz. Like Bach in the *Goldberg Variations*, Herriman creates many interestingly individual variations on his simple-seeming theme, using an array of minor characters: Kolin Kelly, "dealer in bricks"; the stork who brings children; Krazy's fish and bird counterparts; Ignatz's wife; and various citizens of and visitors to Coconino County.

No doubt Herriman's images, as much as those of any modernist, had personal sources, and perhaps also art-historical precedents. But whereas it seems appropriate to interpret museum work with such tools, the wonderful 3 September 1916 episode of *Krazy Kat* (Fig. 16), showing Ignatz pursuing Krazy up and down waves—mountainous waves in Arizona!—until finally, the water calmed, they both sleep, does not readily inspire

29. Richard Shiff, *Cézanne and the End of Impressionism* (Chicago: University of Chicago Press, 1984), xiii.

30. Seldes, "The Krazy Kat That Walks by Himself," 207.

31. See Rey, *Les spectres de la bande*, 96–104.

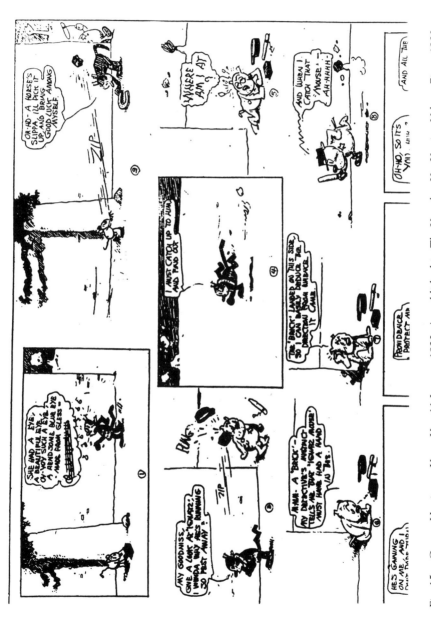

Fig. 15. George Herriman, *Krazy Kat*, 11 January 1920. As published in *The Komplete Kat Komics: Volume Five—1920* (Forestville, Calif.: Eclipse Books, 1990). © King Features.

Fig. 16.   George Herriman, *Krazy Kat*, 3 September 1916. As published in *The Komplete Kat Komics: Volume One—1916* (Forestville, Calif.: Eclipse Books, 1988). © King Features.

search for sources. Perhaps Herriman looked at Dutch seascapes or knew Hokusai's famous wave, but it seems heavy-handed to seek his iconography or to ask the "meaning" of his tale: Krazy never asks why he enjoys being hit by bricks; nor does Offissa Pupp question his role. This is typical of comics: Batman is always brave; Superman, almost always invulnerable. Lack of development, one source of the feeling that comics are too simple to be serious art, is offset by the multiplicity of variations on a given theme. Repetitions of pleasurable violence mean that Ignatz, Krazy, and Offissa Pupp, who never learn, are less like many novelistic characters than drives in the psyche, or the will as it was characterized by Schopenhauer.

Why would a cat love a mouse and enjoy punishment; why should a dog protect a cat? To these questions there is no interesting answer, but once we accept this absurd situation, everything else follows. In Picasso, we use art-historical materials to interpret visual fantasy as a private revelation. *La Vie* (1903), a deeply enigmatic work to which John Richardson's *Life of Picasso* devotes ten pages, calls for analysis. "Mystery is intrinsic to the painting's power."[32] But an appeal, say, to Freud's discussion of sadomasochism in order to understand the sources of Herriman's art seems beside the point. It is as if, rather, Herriman is interpreting us, showing us, his public, something of *our* fantasy life. We do not need layers of interpretation, because we learn from his art, not how to understand him, but how to view ourselves. What we see revealed in *Krazy Kat* is not Herriman's but our very own fantasies. The Chardin of southern California, Herriman is a great poetic celebrant of the minor everyday frustrations and the lasting pleasures of posthistorical domestic life.

Like Gary Larson, Herriman also makes his reader laugh, but his is a more benign imagination. In the tradition of pastoral landscape, he sets his strips in Arcadia, an ideal place outside or at the end of history. To the extent that we imaginatively become Herriman's characters, the words spoken by the figure in Poussin's *Arcadian Shepherds*—"I, too, was born, in Arcadia"—could be said also by us, for we too are momentarily set outside history. Ignatz's nasty aggressiveness, tamed by Krazy's good humor, yields social harmony. If Offissa Pupp does not succeed, still he never succumbs to despair; nor does Kat get bored with his futile love for Ignatz. For all of their obvious imperfections, the three of them carry on happily. And that, I think, is why they inspire ready identification from many very different

---

32. John Richardson, *A Life of Picasso* (New York: Random House, 1991), 1:270.

readers. Like any creative person who successfully sublimates his obsessions, Herriman uses repetition to create pleasure. In Krazy's world, there
is not much work, apart from brick making and an occasional bit of farm-
ing and retail selling. There is no development and no progress. We have
what W. H. Auden, in his account of Eden, calls "temporal novelty . . .
without anxiety, temporal repetition without boredom."[33]

Of course, I am not contending that George Herriman or Winsor
McCay or the other inventors of the modern comic understood their cre-
ations in these, my philosopher's, terms. Their entire concern, I am sure,
was immediate and practical. The newspaper owners of the day desired
quickly drawn, visually attractive content, and these cartoonists used the
resources of visual art to satisfy this demand. Like the contemporary
movie producers or the great rock-and-roll musicians of the 1960s, these
cartoonists hardly needed or were prepared to offer bookish characteriza-
tions of their activity. The properly philosophical dimension of their work
arises only when it is set in historical perspective. My description of the
comics, running far outside any description of their intentions that the
artists could immediately recognize, stands to their everyday concerns
much as Arthur Danto's analysis of Andy Warhol's *Brillo Box* stands to
the everyday world of pop art as revealed by Bob Colacello, whose utterly
absorbing *Holy Terror: Andy Warhol Close Up* has no more need of explicitly philosophical analysis than Saint-Simon's very Proustian *Mémoires*,
a not entirely dissimilar close-up study of hustling, social climbing, and
snobbery in which the concerns of philosophers seem to be absolutely
over the horizon.

Presented philosophically in my poor analytic description, comics seem
elaborate, even a little cumbersome. Were someone who had never seen
a comic to read this description, they would think: what an odd Rube
Goldberg visual apparatus. What then seems astonishing, and marks the
legitimate distance of philosophical analysis from everyday life, is that
when comics developed, they were understood immediately by everyone.

33. W. H. Auden, "Arcadia and Utopia," in *The Dyer's Hand and Other Essays* (New York:
Random House, 1962), 409–11.

PART THREE

THE PLACE OF COMICS IN
RELATION TO ART HISTORY

POSTHISTORICAL ART;
OR, COMICS AND THE
REALM OF
ABSOLUTE KNOWLEDGE

CHAPTER
7

IN ART WE HAVE TO DEAL, NOT WITH ANY AGREEABLE OR USEFUL
CHILD'S PLAY, BUT WITH THE LIBERATION OF THE SPIRIT FROM THE
CONTENT AND FORMS OF FINITUDE, WITH THE PRESENCE AND
RECONCILIATION OF THE ABSOLUTE IN WHAT IS APPARENT AND VISIBLE,
WITH AN UNFOLDING OF THE TRUTH WHICH IS NOT EXHAUSTED IN
NATURAL HISTORY BUT REVEALED IN WORLD-HISTORY.

—HEGEL, AESTHETICS: LECTURES ON FINE ART

"I want to speak," Baudelaire writes in "Some French Caricaturists"
(1855), "about a man who each morning keeps the populace of our city
amused, a man who supplies the daily needs of public gaiety and provides
its sustenance. The bourgeois, the business-man, the urchin and the
housewife all laugh and pass their way, as often as not—what base ingrati-
tude!—without even glancing at his name." It has taken a while, he adds,
to recognize that Daumier "is really the proper subject for a study."[1] Even
today, proper study of successful caricaturists and comics artists has barely
begun. For all of their commercial success, they have, still, an oddly marginal role in art history.[2]

1. Baudelaire, *The Painter of Modern Life*, 171.
2. See also Rey, *Les spectres de la bande*. Kunzle's interesting remarks about the seeming para-
dox of Goethe's interest in Töpffer perhaps make too much of Goethe's conservative politics,
which has some affinities with Baudelaire's (David Kunzle, "Goethe and Caricature: From Hogarth to Töpffer," *Journal of the Warburg and Courtauld Institutes* 48 [1985]: 164–88). Töpffer's
image sequences anticipate Baudelaire's prose poems, modernist narratives using themes from
everyday life, without classical allusions.

When writing my book on Baudelaire, *High Art: Charles Baudelaire and the Origins of Modernism* (1996), I was struck by the way that, as early as his "Salon of 1846," he describes two distinctly different kinds of art: the classical work of Delacroix and the painting of modern life. The modernist tradition was established, so it turned out in ways Baudelaire died too early to understand, by his friend Manet. That Baudelaire doesn't have any sense of how this seemingly discontinuous transition, which from our vantage point marks the origin of modernism, should be described is unsurprising. Right when a transition is happening, how can it possibly be fully understood? We too live in an age of transition, I argued in *High Art*. But in identifying Baudelaire's criticism as relevant also to our situation, I did not say anything about his pioneering analysis of caricature. And yet his own transition from a theological analysis of laughter to the remarkable anticipation of recent concerns with popular art forms is as odd a transition as that in the "Salon of 1846" from Delacroix's correspondences to the painting of modern life. When taking up the much discussed idea that Baudelaire anticipated Impressionism, I failed to say what to a student of comics ought to be obvious—that his discussions of caricature and the narrative structure of *Le spleen de Paris* anticipated comics. But here we get to ideas that deserve a more extended exposition.

How do comics begin? The origin of some art forms is hard to explain. Why was caricature developed only in the seventeenth century, when the techniques of image making had long been highly sophisticated? These techniques were available, but they were not used earlier. The "controlled regression" essential to caricature, Ernst Kris and E. H. Gombrich plausibly argue, is possible only when "aggression has remained in the aesthetic sphere and thus we react not with hostility but with laughter."[3] Their analysis must remain speculative; it relies upon indirect evidence and not upon any detailed and explicit verbal statements by the artists themselves. Analogously, why was it only in the early twentieth century that the comic strip was developed, when the techniques of balloons and image sequences had long been available? That question is easy to answer. Only when newspapers needed to attract a newly literate mass audience was there reason to make these images. Once that need was felt, it was easily satisfied; the invention of comics required only adaptation of an already existing visual technology, the speech balloon, and development of the closely linked narrative sequence.

3. Ernst Kris and E. H. Gombrich, "The Principles of Caricature," in *Psychoanalytic Explorations in Art*, by Ernst Kris (London: George Allen & Unwin, 1953), 197, 203.

To understand the history of the comic strip, we need to go back to Gombrich's argument about the development of representation presented in the Introduction, now reading his claims in relation to Arthur C. Danto's recent discussions of the end of art's history. For an art form to have an autonomous history, it must in some way develop its own visual concerns. Formalists and Gombrich agree: the history of European painting does not reduce to its social history. As Sydney Freedberg writes, "We may in part interpret Cinquecento classicism as a solution, in terms of art that *do not touch political reality, and are not essentially touched by it,* to the Quattrocento's cultural dilemma" (my italics).[4]

A nonformalist Gombrichian history of painting from Cimabue to Pissarro is possible because there was progress in representation making; a social history supplements that account, explaining why this particular culture encouraged such experimentation. But caricature and comics, arts based upon conventions, cannot have an autonomous history of that sort. Recent comics artists have developed styles different from those of Winsor McCay and George Herriman, but once the word balloon and the narrative sequence were invented, the basic tools of this art form were available. The presentation of novel content did not require any additions to or radical development of these techniques. In this sense, there is no progress in comics—there are no deep ways in which present-day balloons or image sequences differ in kind from those of the pioneering artists. This is why histories of comics do not take the form of Vasari's *Lives* or Gombrich's *Story of Art*—these histories are, rather, stories of a succession of personalities who have used this medium in individual ways.

Film, created at the same time as comics, also depends upon novel technologies, but unlike comics the movies really are a completely new art form. Development of the early silent films triggered further sweeping technical innovations. Theoreticians then had to describe the role of sound and color—novel techniques that were sometimes felt to transform that art entirely or even to destroy it. According to Arnheim, writing in 1930, "Even if it should be possible to perfect the technology of colored film, nothing will have been gained. Rather, one of those qualities of the camera that makes film art possible will have been lost."[5] McCay and some other comics artists were actively involved with animated films, but

4. Freedberg, *Painting in Italy*, 3.

5. Rudolf Arnheim, *Film Essays and Criticism*, trans. Brenda Benthien (Madison: University of Wisconsin Press, 1997), 13.

their comic strips did not require such radical technical innovation. Already in 1906, Lyonel Feininger's *Kin-der-Kids* featured "a full-fledged, frankly suspenseful week-to-week narrative continuity."[6] Recently, very long strips, even some multivolume works, have been made, but mere length does not, I would argue, change the nature of this medium. These strips are but lengthened versions of the early comics.[7]

Many recent comics artists are highly innovative. Art Spiegelman's *Maus* transcends the boundaries of the traditional comic—in place of the repetitive narrative based on the daily strip, we have a story with flashbacks, as complex a narrative as that in novels.[8] And when, to mention but one example, it presents Jews as mice who can wear face masks to pose as Polish pigs but may be uncovered by the German cats, it displays genuine visual invention. The David Mairowitz/Robert Crumb life of Kafka also presents a seriously original theme in a comic.[9] Paul Auster's *City of Glass* presents a complex crime story, and Archie Rand and other visual artists have made comics using original imagery.[10] *Chiaroscuro* tells the life of Leonardo da Vinci à la Freud in highly imaginative ways (Fig. 17). And Osamu Tezuka presents a fully achieved historical fiction, a story about 1930s fascism (Fig. 18). But none of these important artists has changed the essence of their medium—they all use word balloons and narrative sequences to tell stories visually in book-size formats. What is deserving of the highest praise is their introduction of original content and styles of storytelling into this medium, whose essential properties remain unchanged. But here we return to one leitmotiv of this book. Comics must be evaluated in their own terms. To treat comic strips as small modernist paintings with words added would be unfair when in fact their essence—so also their history—is very different.

6. Bill Blackbeard, ed., *The Complete Comic Strip Art of Lyonel Feininger* (Northampton, Mass.: Kitchen Sink Press, 1994), 4.

7. Danto's reply to my earlier wrongheaded criticism of his position helped me to see the importance of defining an art (Arthur C. Danto, *After the End of Art: Contemporary Art and the Pale of History* [Princeton: Princeton University Press, 1997], 193–98; David Carrier, "Gombrich and Danto on Defining Art," *Journal of Aesthetics and Art Criticism* 54, no. 3 [1996]: 279–81; idem, "Introduction: Danto and His Critics: Art History, Historiography, and *After the End of Art*," *History and Theory*, Theme Issue 37 [1998]: 1–16).

8. Art Spiegelman, *Maus* (New York: Pantheon, 1986) and idem, *Maus II: A Survivor's Tale: And Here My Troubles Began* (New York: Pantheon, 1991).

9. David Zane Mairowitz and Robert Crumb, *Introducing Kafka* (Northampton, Mass.: Kitchen Sink Press, 1994).

10. Paul Auster, *City of Glass*, adaptation by Paul Karasik and David Mazzucchelli, graphics by David Mazzucchelli (New York: Avon, 1994); Archie Rand (artist) and John Yau (writer), *Mug City Moves* (New York: A Monkey Choir, Maestros Production, 1991).

Fig. 17.   *Chiaroscuro: The Private Lives of Leonardo da Vinci. Chiaroscuro 3*, published
by DC Comics. © 1995 Pat McGreal, David Rawson, and Chas Truog. All
rights reserved. Used with permission.

Fig. 18. Osamu Tezuka, *Adolf: An Exile in Japan*. © Tezuka Productions.

New artistic media have recently been created. The 1960s conceptual and performance art and earthworks, and some recent work with personal computers, are art forms whose defining qualities remain, as yet, incompletely identified. But once Richard Outcault learned how to ink in the color for his *Yellow Kid*, all the essential technology required for comics existed. Comics artists added to the techniques of representation practiced by properly trained nineteenth-century painters systematic use of the speech balloon and narrative sequences; and those additions do not allow or demand either the kind of formal innovations discussed by Sydney Freedberg or the making and matching that defines a Gombrichian history of representation. A history of the comics must therefore be a social history—an account of the ways in which this art form reflects changing social and political goals and needs.[11]

A great avant-garde painter like Mondrian, whose importance only became generally apparent after his death, could lead a marginal life; a comics writer needs an audience. (Even Herriman, who appeared in a small number of newspapers, was—thanks to William Randolph Hearst's personal love of his art—seen by more people than all but the most famous "serious" artists.) "Television is still highly transparent," Alexander Nehamas writes, and so it "convinces us on many occasion that what we see *in* it is precisely what we see *through* it."[12] Comics also remain transparent, and their history reveals how much shared values have changed. Informed by the just demands of a multicultural 1990s society, we look with displeasure at the racism of early strips and the assumptions made about women's social roles; erotic imagery, found early on repressed in crude under-the-table strips, appeared openly in 1960s underground publications. But all of these changes in comics' content have not been accompanied by any dramatic developments in their visual technology.

How different is the situation in art history proper. A history of modernist painting must deal with cubism, surrealism, various forms of realism, abstract expressionism, minimalism, and pop art. The 1950s art of Robert Ryman, like the 1960s paintings of Robert Mangold and Andy Warhol or Sean Scully's work of the 1980s, would have been incomprehensible to a Paris audience of 1905. To understand these artworks is impossible with-

11. See Berger, *The Comic-Stripped American*.

12. Alexander Nehamas, "Plato and the Mass Media," *Monist* 71 (spring 1988): 227. He is commenting on Danto's idea that "a literary work is about its readers" in a metaphorical way (Arthur C. Danto, *The Philosophical Disenfranchisement of Art* [New York: Columbia University Press, 1986], 155).

out knowing the story of modernism.[13] By contrast, although McCay and Herriman might be a little surprised by the content of Robert Crumb's or Osamu Tezuka's comics, they would have no difficulty understanding these artists' techniques. Comics stand to museum art rather as pop recording does to classical music; once the early rock-and-roll pioneers discovered how to perform Afro-American blues on electric instruments, the essentials of that art had been identified. The interesting discoveries were made very early on, Robert Johnson's 1930s recordings employing, in technically primitive form, almost all of the musical techniques that made the Rolling Stones famous in the 1960s.

The same point can be made about caricature: Daumier had already mastered what remain the essential techniques of present-day caricaturists. Like comics, caricature remains today as good as it was when it began; these two arts have not advanced (or declined), because they are not in need of essential new discoveries. When in his *Lives* Vasari famously speaks of how the "arts resemble nature . . . and have their birth, growth, age and death," so that Giotto came to obscure the glory of Cimabue—

> Cimabue thought
> To lord it over painting's field; and now
> The cry is Giotto's, and his name eclips'd

—his account, however much it has been recently questioned, is a very natural way of describing the whole of European art history from that time through to Impressionism.[14] Nothing like that can be said about comic strips or caricature; more recent comics artists do not stand in this sort of relation to McCay or Herriman. One of the reasons that comics are difficult to analyze is that the working tools of art historians are designed to deal with historical development. Perhaps comics are thought marginal because in art we expect progress. Think how much attention we give to radical innovators, and what qualified praise it is to say of someone that she or he only works skillfully in a traditional way. But the most famous comics illustrators were boldly original not in terms of their formal innovations but because they found new subjects and original kinds

13. See David Carrier, "Robert Mangold, *Gray Window Wall* (1964)," *Burlington Magazine* 138 (December 1996): 826–28; idem, "Andy Warhol's Moving Pictures of Modern Life," *Source* 16, no. 3 (1997): 30–34; and idem, "Robert Ryman on the Origins of His Art."
14. Vasari, *The Lives of the Painters*, 1:18, 27.

of characters. In this way, these creators of comics seem more like novelists than visual artists.

In a wonderfully suggestive series of now justly famous texts, Danto argues that ours is a posthistorical era, a time in which, as he puts it in his 1995 A. W. Mellon lectures, "the history of art, structured narratively, has come to an end."[15] Everything is possible, he argues, because no longer is there a direction to history. This is a dramatic change, for in both the old-master era discussed by Gombrich and modernism as presented by Clement Greenberg, periods of sudden radical innovation were expected to reoccur regularly. Danto argues that Robert Mangold's *Yellow Wall (Section* I + II) (1964) (Fig. 19) and Warhol's *Brillo Box,* a sculpture of the same year, are artifacts that, because they are visually indistinguishable from mere things, mark the end of the historical development of art. Perhaps only an aesthetician's theory can remove Mangold's and Warhol's objects far enough away from us to make it obvious that they indeed are artworks. This collapse of the distance between art and everyday things yields, Danto argues, a Hegelian lesson. When there is no gap between knowledge and its object, then "knowledge is its own object, hence subject and object at once."[16] Posthistorical art ends painting's development by closing that gap between the arts and philosophy.

Whatever the ultimate judgment on Danto's account, it provides a perfect historiographical perspective on comics, which have, since they were created, always existed in a posthistorical era. Their history lacks a developmental structure, for what they are now they were already in the beginning. New themes have been added, and they reflect changing social mores, but their essential structure has remained fixed.[17] Looking backward, viewing the history of art in light of the historical perspective I have supplied, comics appear the natural end point of the tradition of European painting. Making outwardly visible the inner feelings of depicted figures, unambiguously presenting the development of action: when these goals are fully achieved by comics, then the whole tradition from Giotto through Impressionism finds its natural resolution—or, rather, one resolution, for unlike Danto I think that there is more than one way to tell the story of art's history.

Danto resists the suggestion that we can relativize talk of endings by

15. Danto, *After the End of Art,* 126.
16. Danto, *The Philosophical Disenfranchisement of Art.*
17. For example, the story of Tintin in Africa was, for political reasons, not translated; see Hergé, *Les aventures de Tintin: Tintin au Congo* (Paris: Casterman, 1974).

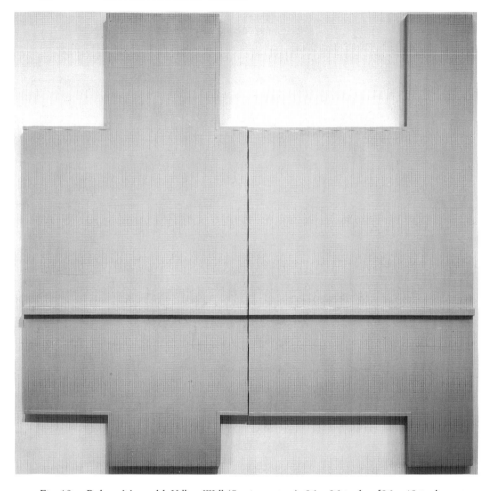

Fig. 19.   Robert Mangold, *Yellow Wall (Section* I + II), 96 x 96 inches [96 x 48 inches, two panels], 1964. Courtesy of PaceWildenstein.

allowing that one narrative has ended but another story goes on. A realist about historiography, he speaks of "objective narrative structures in the way human events unfold," identifying the ending of his story of art's history with the ending of *the* story, not just an ending of a particular narrative.[18] There is a familiar division between Continental and analytic

18. Danto, *After the End of Art,* 101. See David Carrier, "Danto as Systematic Philosopher; or, *Comme on lit Danto en français,*" in *Arthur Danto and His Critics,* ed. M. Rollins (Cambridge, Mass.: Basil Blackwell, 1993), 13–27, and idem, "Introduction: Danto and His Critics."

philosophers—between those who think that the accounts of the narrative only describe mere texts and those who argue that such texts describe
the world as it really is in itself. Danto takes the viewpoint of analytic
philosophers. For him, it is unacceptable to allow that he has told the end
of one history of art while other narratives tell an ongoing story. As an
analytic philosopher of action, he has spoken of identifying the same
action differently under different descriptions. Appealing to his concept
of a "basic action," an action "we do but not *through* any distinct thing
which we also do," he argues: "A man blesses someone by raising his arm.
The blessing is something he does *through* raising his arm, and so seems
non-basic, but clearly there is no event distinct from the raising of the arm
in which the blessing consists. . . . we have . . . a basic action performed in
conformity with a rule which licenses a redescription of it as a blessing."[19]
As G. E. M. Anscombe writes in her classic account of intention, one
source for Danto's analysis: "[T]he same action can be intentional under
one description and unintentional under another."[20] But Danto has no
tolerance for pluralistic narratology. Danto's Hegelian historicism and es-
sentialism about the nature of art are compatible only if art's history has
ended. Only now, when nothing essentially new is possible, can we survey
the field of art, which we can characterize completely because it cannot
expand to encompass novel kinds of artifacts. Often relativism and historicism are linked together, but Danto, though a historicist, is not a relativ-
ist. What is discovered through art's development, he believes, is its
essence.

On Danto's straightforward characterization of their activity, "historians . . . try to make true statements, or to give true descriptions, of events
in *their* past."[21] This is what he himself does when writing as an art critic.
So long as there are additional events that amount to something more
than endgame moves, further history is possible. Insofar as the goal of the
historian, so he taught us in *Analytic Philosophy of History*, is to write
narrative sentences, a further history can be written so long as there are
more events to describe. Danto the art critic keeps writing, while Danto
the aesthetician asserts that the history of art has come to an end. Can
the grand philosophical history of art told by Gombrich, Greenberg, and
Danto end, while we have new histories describing Robert Mapplethorpe,

19. Arthur C. Danto, *Analytical Philosophy of Action* (Cambridge: Cambridge University Press,
1973), 28, 29.
20. G. E. M. Anscombe, *Intention* (Oxford: Basil Blackwell, 1957), 28.
21. Danto, *Narration and Knowledge*, 25.

Sean Scully, Mark Tansey, and the many other recent artists Danto has written about? This conciliatory way of talking amounts to saying that the history of art continues under one description but not under another. If the story of art is identified with the history of the discovery of its essential properties, the story told by Plato, Kant, Hegel, Heidegger, and also Gombrich and Greenberg, then—if we accept Danto's analysis—that history ended with *Brillo Box*. But why must this very interesting narrative be *the* history of art? Danto's ontological history ends because the field of potential art objects expands to include any kind of object. Anything could be an artwork once it was discovered that being an artwork is not defined by a thing's visual properties; being an artwork requires being about something and embodying its meaning, as *Brillo Box* does. This argument is not necessarily inconsistent with my neo-Gombrichian history of representation, which ends in the comic strip. We may, if we want, privilege Danto's account by calling it *the* philosophical history of art. But that, in my opinion, is merely a verbal concession.

After the End of Art carries the historical analysis further than Gombrich and Greenberg, building upon their intuition that what art history requires is a narrative history, but outflanking them by showing how their histories of art were demonstrated by Warhol to be incomplete. In *Artwriting* (1987), a book dedicated to Danto, I pointed to the problems inherent in Gombrich's master narrative of making and matching, in which Duccio leads ultimately to Constable. That account foregrounds the development of representation and leaves in the background changes in the function and social role of art. Claiming that this Gombrichian analysis is *the* story of art requires highly selective reading of the evidence and a positively Hegelian downplaying of artists' intentions. As Paul Barolsky has suggested to me, "The story of art is really lots and lots of very particular stories." Greenberg's master narrative about modernism, in which the self-criticality of Manet and his successors leads to cubism and on to Pollock, requires omission of Salon art, Rodin, the Pre-Raphaelites, most of Picasso, Morandi, Giacometti, German expressionism, futurism, Dada and surrealism, photography, American realism, and much more. (His selective account is justified, Greenberg believed, because what he leaves out mostly is relatively minor art.) Danto urges that in his posthistorical era pluralism is possible, but already in Greenberg's era that was true; the more the history of modernism is rewritten, the clearer it will be that art's situation for a long time was already posthistorical.

Has not Danto the historiographer taught us that any history must be

selective, setting events into a pattern, as when Gombrich, at the end of
Art and Illusion, can bring in abstract art only via an oddly ad hoc analysis
of caricature? Danto overestimates the intrinsic strength of these developmental narratives—a procedure that accounts for some of the drama he
creates by juxtaposing against them his own history. I have more problems
than he does treating *Art and Illusion* and *Art and Culture* as literally
true, rather than as great quasi-fictions—hence my problems also with his
realism. But that is a disagreement about a mere detail. My aim here is
not to criticize Gombrich or Greenberg, but to praise them. How admirable were their wills to interpret, which permitted them to construct lucid
narratives from bewildering incomplete evidence. I praise Danto and call
him the logical successor of Gombrich and Greenberg, for the same reason. But in thus praising these three great art-historical historiographers,
I deny Danto's claim that he is describing history as it really is and not
merely offering one imaginative reading of the evidence.

That is an abstract argument. What really is called for by Danto's critics
is the construction of alternative histories. Just as in the Introduction I
borrowed from Gombrich while rejecting his view of the historical place
of caricature, so here I employ Danto's happily pregnant conception of
posthistorical art while denying his reading of history. For me, as for Alexander Nehamas's Nietzsche, "there is no single best narrative. . . . What
is best is always determined in light of different background assumptions,
interests, and values; and none of these can make an exclusive claim to
being perfectly and objectively valid—valid for all."[22] To understand the
implications of that view for my history of comics, additional philosophical analysis is called for.

At the very end of history, in the stage of what he calls Absolute
Knowledge, Hegel explains that "the negation of the object, its canceling
its own existence, gets, for self-consciousness, a positive significance; or,
self-consciousness knows this nothingness of the object because on the
one hand self-consciousness itself externalizes itself; for in doing so it
establishes itself as object, or, by reason of the indivisible unity characterizing its self-existence, sets up the object as its self."[23] As he noted in his
lectures on aesthetics, "the spirit only occupies itself with objects so long

22. Alexander Nehamas, *Nietzsche: Life as Literature* (Cambridge, Mass.: Harvard University
Press, 1985), 100.
23. G. W. F. Hegel, *The Phenomenology of Mind,* trans. J. B. Baillie (New York: Harper & Row,
1967), 789.

as there is something secret, not revealed in them."[24] At this end of history, in the materialist rewriting of Hegel by Marx and Engels in *The German Ideology*, we come to the abolition of division of labor and the state that makes it possible "to hunt in the morning, fish in the afternoon, rear cattle in the evening, criticize after dinner, just as I have a mind, without ever becoming hunter, fisherman, shepherd, or critic."[25] In this posthistorical culture, when "there is nothing new in the world," we find what Alexandre Kojève calls "the ceasing of action in a strong sense of the term," and what then remains is "art, love, play, etc.—in short, all that makes man happy."[26]

The association of the end of historical conflict (and art) with play is, of course, a traditional theme in German philosophy. Schiller, for example, wrote: "All other forms of perception divide man, because they are founded exclusively either upon the sensuous or upon the spiritual part of his being; only the aesthetic mode of perception makes of him a whole, because both his natures must be in harmony if he is to achieve it."[27] What is new in Marx's account is the idea that such play might displace the unending conflicts of earlier cultural history and become *the* social activity. The end of art's history, as Danto and I understand it, is by no means the end of history as such, as Kojève and his follower Francis Fukuyama claim; everything I say about comics is perfectly consistent with developing a critical leftist analysis of this art form, such as is provided by Ariel Dorfman's admirably forceful accounts.[28] Perhaps history itself will continue even if art's history ends; the reasons Hegel and Marx gave for linking these histories may no longer inspire conviction, but this observation says nothing about the validity of Danto's more narrowly focused argument about Andy Warhol.

No doubt it is extravagant to read these far-reaching speculations as describing comics, an art form unknown to Hegel, as extravagant as it was

24. Hegel, *Aesthetics: Lectures on Fine Art*, 1:604.

25. Karl Marx and Friedrich Engels, *Basic Writings on Politics and Philosophy*, ed. Lewis S. Feuer (Garden City, N.Y.: Anchor Books, 1959), 254; see also David Carrier, "Art Criticism and the Death of Marxism," *Leonardo* 30, no. 3 (1997): 241–45.

26. Alexandre Kojève, *Introduction à la lecture de Hegel* (Paris: Gallimard, 1947), 443, 435.

27. Friedrich Schiller, *On the Aesthetic Education of Man*, trans. Elizabeth M. Wilkinson and L. A. Willoughby (Oxford: Clarendon Press, 1967), 215.

28. See Ariel Dorfman, *The Empire's Old Clothes: What the Lone Ranger, Babar, and Other Innocent Heroes Do to Our Minds* (New York: Pantheon, 1983), and Ariel Dorfman and Armand Mattelart, *How to Read Donald Duck: Imperialist Ideology in the Disney Comic*, translated, with an introduction, by David Kunzle (New York: International General, 1975).

for Marx to declare that the account of Spirit's coming to self-consciousness was really about the end of class struggle, or for Kojève to pronounce
that the end of history was reached in 1950s America (and Japan). Like
these Continental philosophers, Danto has become a gloriously speculative historical thinker—what an odd role for an analytic philosopher! But
what links all of these accounts of the end of political struggle to theorizing about the end of art's history is the shared conception that when there
no longer is any separation between knowing subject and known object,
then all knowledge is only—what else can it then be?—self-knowledge.
Spirit, so Hegel tells, "appears in time so long as it does not grasp its pure
notion, i.e. so long as it does not annul time. Time is the pure self in
external form."[29] When this is recognized, then history, the process of
temporal development, necessarily has ended. In Danto's ontological
analysis, the history of art comes to an end because Duchamp's ready-
mades and Warhol's *Brillo Box* show that any sort of object can, in the
right circumstances, enter the museum. In my historical analysis, the development of comics marks a posthistorical phase of art history because
this art form, not needing or being able to progress, abolishes the distance
between subject and object. As I read Hegel, that jargon is a way of saying
that the interpretation of comics requires only that knowledge which
everyone possesses.

Many commentators have worried that in Danto's posthistorical period
art making will cease to be a challenging activity. When everything has
been done, can artists continue to work seriously? Fukuyama's Hegelian-
Nietzschean *End of History and the Last Man*, without reference to Danto,
claims that a posthistorical era "will mean the end . . . of all art that could
be considered socially useful, and hence the descent of artistic activity
into the empty formalism of the traditional Japanese arts."[30] We have, as
yet, few ways of prophesying the structure of such posthistorical periods,
but I think this pessimism premature. A posthistorical art form can be
very lively indeed—think of the intense interest comics art has recently
generated in its use of the traditional narrative sequence and word balloon
to present new subjects. Danto's account is an ontological history of art—
and he is correct to conclude that this argument shows that the field of
art can expand no further. But this identification of the role of Warhol's
Brillo Box is entirely consistent with other descriptions of the history of

29. Hegel, *The Phenomenology of Mind*, 800.
30. Francis Fukuyama, *The End of History and the Last Man* (New York: Free Press, 1992), 320.

art in which the ending is located at another moment or has not yet occurred and may, for all we know, never occur. Given Danto's association of posthistorical art with play, it seems appropriate that comics, an essentially playful art, can so naturally be fitted into his account. That comics belong to a posthistorical art world does not mean that they are a trivial art form. McCloud, recognizing that the comic has thus far mostly been a marginalized art form, correctly argues that "today the possibilities for comics are—as they always have been—endless."[31] My present discussion supports his claim.

One critical reader of an earlier presentation of my view of mass culture presented in Chapter 6 spoke scornfully of my invocation of "a superior epistemology." If that was the impression given, then that discussion was badly confused, for what I want to do—here I borrow Wittgenstein's characterization of his philosophical investigation—is "to *understand* something that is already in plain view."[32] In comics "self-consciousness itself externalizes itself . . . it establishes itself as object, or, by reason of the indivisible unity characterizing its self-existence, sets up the object as its self."[33] After so many serious interpretations of Hegel, why not allow also this very serious, frankly comic reading of his argument? *Krazy Kat* provides the best picture I can imagine of life in a posthistorical world.

Does this seem like a great weight to place upon these slight images? Comic strips are hard to get into proper focus. "Aesthetics has a reach far wider than the preoccupation with art as such," Danto has written; "it would be . . . an immense contribution to the understanding of ourselves as cognitive beings if we were to study . . . the extent to which we are aesthetic beings."[34] This is exactly what, in my view, comics do. It seems to me appropriate that this theory of comics itself is comic. But then my defect as commentator, so reviewers say, is that I do not know when to stop. "Carrier the writer is, like Poussin the painter, one who actively chooses to write in a Talmudic way."[35] We two gentiles, Poussin and I, writing and painting as Jews—I laughed when I read this comic characterization of us. Relating Herriman's humble works to these far-reaching

31. McCloud, *Understanding Comics*, 212.
32. Ludwig Wittgenstein, *Philosophical Investigations*, trans. G. E. M. Anscombe (New York: Macmillan, 1953), 42.
33. Hegel, *The Phenomenology of Mind*, 799.
34. Arthur C. Danto, *Embodied Meanings: Critical Essays and Aesthetic Meditations* (New York: Farrrar, Straus & Giroux, 1994), 382, 383.
35. Daniel Herwitz, review of *Poussin's Paintings*, by David Carrier, *Journal of Aesthetics and Art Criticism* 53, no. 3 (1995): 327.

speculations, associating a man whose friends were L.A. film writers with Hegel, Heidegger, and Wittgenstein—no doubt I am going too far. But where is the proper stopping point when theorizing about what is close at hand? It is in part because, judged by the standards of visual art in the museum, they seem slight, that Herriman's comics are so interesting to the philosopher of art. This book has tried to show why a slight-seeming art is of great philosophical interest.

But here I really do exceed my brief, for my real goal in praising work that has given me great pleasure was to explain why I think it deserves your attention as well. A commentator on the comics inevitably runs the risk of being like the fan to whom Herriman wrote, in response to his letter of inquiry: "Your strange interest in my efforts sure has me in a quandary—yes sir I can't add it up at all—It must be something you give to it."[36]

36. Quoted in McDonnell, O'Connell, and Riley de Havenon, *Krazy Kat*, 25. On the influence of Herriman, see Berkson, *Homage to George Herriman*.

BIBLIOGRAPHY

A full bibliography of the comics literature would be enormous. This partial account-ing of the books I have consulted is highly selective. Not every item here is footnoted in the text. I do not duplicate the bibliographies in my earlier books.

Abbott, Lawrence L. "Comic Art: Characteristics and Potentialities of a Narrative Medium." *Journal of Popular Culture* 19, no. 4 (1986): 155–76.

Ackroyd, Peter. *T. S. Eliot: A Life*. New York: Simon & Schuster, 1984.

Adelman, Bob, with Art Spiegelman, Richard Merkin, and Madeline Kripke. *Tijuana Bibles: Art and Wit in America's Forbidden Funnies, 1930s–1950s*. New York: Simon & Schuster, 1997.

Andrae, Thomas. "From Menace to Messiah: The Prehistory of Superman in Science Fiction Literature." *Discourse* 2 (summer 1980): 84–111.

Anscombe, G. E. M. *Intention*. Oxford: Basil Blackwell, 1957.

Arnheim, Rudolf. *Film Essays and Criticism*. Translated by Brenda Benthien. Madison: University of Wisconsin Press, 1997.

Auden, W. H. "Arcadia and Utopia." In *The Dyer's Hand and Other Essays*, 409–11. New York: Random House, 1962.

Auster, Paul. *City of Glass*. Adaptation by Paul Karasik and David Mazzucchelli, graph-ics by David Mazzucchelli. New York: Avon, 1994.

Backwords, Ace. *Twisted Image*. Port Townsend, Wash.: Loompanics Unlimited, 1990.

Barolsky, Paul. *Infinite Jest: Wit and Humor in Italian Renaissance Art*. Columbia: Uni-versity of Missouri Press, 1978.

———. *Why Mona Lisa Smiles and Other Tales by Vasari*. University Park: The Pennsyl-vania State University Press, 1991.

Barrier, Michel K., and Martin T. William. *A Smithsonian Book of Comic-Book Comics*. Washington, D.C.: Smithsonian Institution, 1981.

Barthes, Roland. *S/Z*. Translated by Richard Miller. New York: Hill & Wang, 1974.

Bassy, Alain-Marie. "Du texte à l'illustration: Pour une sémiologie des étapes." *Semiot-ica* 2 (1974): 297–324.

Batman Dailies: Volume I, 1943–1944. Princeton, Wis.: Kitchen Sink Press, 1990.

Baudelaire, Charles. *The Painter of Modern Life and Other Essays*. Translated by Jona-than Mayne. London: Phaidon Press, 1964.

———. *The Poems in Prose with "La Fanfarlo."* Translated by Francis Scarfe. London: Anvil Press Poetry, 1989.

Baxandall, Michael. *Patterns of Intention: On the Historical Explanation of Pictures*. New Haven: Yale University Press, 1985.

Becker, Stephen. *Comic Art in America.* New York: Simon & Schuster, 1959.

Benayoun, Robert. *Vroom, Tchac, Zowie: Le ballon dans la bande dessinée.* Paris: André Balland, 1968.

Benjamin, Walter. "The Work of Art in the Age of Mechanical Reproduction." In *Illuminations,* translated by Harry Zohn, 217–51. New York: Schocken, 1969.

Berger, Arthur Asa. *The Comic-Stripped American: What Dick Tracy, Blondie, Daddy Warbucks, and Charlie Brown Tell Us About Ourselves.* Baltimore: Penguin, 1973.

Berkson, Bill. *Homage to George Herriman.* Exhibition catalogue. San Francisco: Campbell-Thiebaud Gallery, 1997.

Blackbeard, Bill. "The Forgotten Years of George Herriman." *Nemo* 1 (1983): 50–60.

———, ed. *The Complete Comic Strip Art of Lyonel Feininger.* Northampton, Mass.: Kitchen Sink Press, 1994.

Brauer, Heinrich, and Rudolf Wittkower. *Die Zeichnungen des Gianlorenzo Bernini.* Berlin: Heinrich Keller, 1931.

Brilliant, Richard. *Visual Narratives: Storytelling in Etruscan and Roman Art.* Ithaca: Cornell University Press, 1984.

Calkins, Robert G. *Illuminated Books of the Middle Ages.* Ithaca: Cornell University Press, 1983.

Calvet, Louis-Jean. *Roland Barthes: A Biography.* Translated by Sarah Wykes. Bloomington: Indiana University Press, 1995.

Camille, Michael. *Image on the Edge: The Margins of Medieval Art.* Cambridge, Mass.: Harvard University Press, 1992.

———. *Master of Death: The Lifeless Art of Pierre Remiet Illuminator.* New Haven: Yale University Press, 1996.

Canemaker, John. *Winsor McCay: His Life and Art.* New York: Abbeville Press, 1987.

Capp, Al. *Li'l Abner Dailies, Volume One: 1934–1936.* Introduction by Catherine Capp Halberstadt. Princeton, Wis.: Kitchen Sink Press, 1988.

Carlin, John, and Sheena Wagstaff. *The Comic Art Show: Cartoons in Painting and Popular Culture.* Exhibition catalogue. New York: Whitney Museum of American Art, 1983.

Carrier, David. "Andy Warhol's Moving Pictures of Modern Life." *Source* 16, no. 3 (1997): 30–34.

———. "Art Criticism and the Death of Marxism." *Leonardo* 30, no. 3 (1997): 241–45.

———. "Art History." In *Contemporary Critical Terms in Art History,* edited by R. Nelson and R. Shiff, 129–41. Chicago: University of Chicago Press, 1996.

———. "Art History in the Mirror Stage: Interpreting *Un Bar aux Folies-Bergère.*" *History and Theory* 29, no. 3 (1990): 297–320.

———. *Artwriting.* Amherst: University of Massachusetts Press, 1987.

———. "Baudelaire's Philosophical Theory of Beauty." *Nineteenth-Century French Studies* 23, nos. 3–4 (spring–summer 1995): 382–402.

———. "The Big Picture: David Carrier Talks with Sir Ernst Gombrich." *Artforum,* February 1996, 66–69, 106, 109.

———. "Blindness and the Representation of Desire in Poussin's Paintings." *res* 19/20 (1990/91): 31–52.

———. "Danto as Systematic Philosopher; or, *Comme on lit Danto en français.*" In *Arthur Danto and His Critics,* edited by M. Rollins, 13–27. Cambridge, Mass.: Basil Blackwell, 1993.

———. "He Dreams She Dreams of Him." In *Puzzles About Art: An Aesthetics Casebook*, edited by M. Battin, J. Fisher, R. Moore, and A. Silvers, 77–78. New York: St. Martins Press, 1989.

———. *High Art: Charles Baudelaire and the Origins of Modernism*. University Park: The Pennsylvania State University Press, 1996.

———. "Gombrich and Danto on Defining Art." *Journal of Aesthetics and Art Criticism* 54, no. 3 (1996): 279–81.

———. "Introduction: Danto and His Critics: Art History, Historiography, and *After the End of Art*." *History and Theory*, Theme Issue 37 (1998): 1–16.

———. "Memory and Oblivion in Contemporary American Art: The Lesson of *Artforum*." In the proceedings of the Twenty-Ninth International Conference on the History of Art, Amsterdam, 1996, forthcoming.

———. "Le opere d'arte false nell'era della riproduzione meccanica." In *Museu dei Musei*, exhibition catalogue, 29–34. Florence: Littauer & Littauer, 1988.

———. "Poussin's Cartesian Meditations: Self and Other in the Self-Portraits of Poussin and Matisse." *Source* 15, no. 3 (1996): 28–35.

———. *Principles of Art History Writing*. University Park: The Pennsylvania State University Press, 1991.

———. "Robert Mangold, *Gray Window Wall* (1964)." *Burlington Magazine* 138 (December 1996): 826–28.

———. "Robert Ryman on the Origins of His Art." *Burlington Magazine* 139 (September 1997): 631–33.

Champfleury. *Son regard et celui de Baudelaire*. Paris: Hermann, 1990.

Clark, T. J. *The Painting of Modern Life: Paris in the Art of Manet and His Followers*. New York: Alfred A. Knopf, 1984.

Coleman, Earle J. "The Funnies, the Movies, and Aesthetics." *Journal of Popular Culture* 18 (1985): 89–100.

The Collected Works of Buck Rogers in the Twenty-Fifth Century. Edited by Robert C. Dille. New York: Chelsea House, 1980.

Couperie, Pierre. *Le noir et blanc dans la bande dessinée*. Paris: Editions Serg, 1974.

Couperie, Pierre, et al. *A History of the Comic Strip*. Translated by Eileen B. Hennessy. New York: Crown, 1974.

Crafton, Donald. *Before Mickey: The Animated Film, 1898–1928*. Cambridge, Mass.: MIT Press, 1982.

Crary, Jonathan. *Techniques of the Observer: On Vision and Modernity in the Nineteenth Century*. Cambridge, Mass.: MIT Press, 1990.

Crumb, Robert. *The Complete Crumb Comics, Volume 4: Mr. Sixties*. Seattle: Fantagraphics Books, 1989.

———. *R. Crumb's Head Comix*. New York: Simon & Schuster, 1988.

Curnow, Wystan. "Speech Balloons and Conversation Bubbles." *And* 4 (October 1985): 125–48.

Danto, Arthur C. *After the End of Art: Contemporary Art and the Pale of History*. Princeton: Princeton University Press, 1997.

———. *Analytical Philosophy of Action*. Cambridge: Cambridge University Press, 1973.

———. "The Artworld." *Journal of Philosophy* 61 (October 1964): 571–84.

———. "Beautiful Science and the Future of Criticism." In *The Future of Literary Theory*, edited by Ralph Cohen, 370–85. New York: Routledge, Chapman & Hall, 1989.

————. *Connections to the World: The Basic Concepts of Philosophy*. Berkeley and Los Angeles: University of California Press, 1997.

————. *Embodied Meanings: Critical Essays and Aesthetic Meditations*. New York: Farrar, Straus & Giroux, 1994.

————. "Giotto and the Stench of Lazarus." *Antaeus* 54 (spring 1985): 7–20.

————. *Narration and Knowledge*. New York: Columbia University Press, 1985.

————. *The Philosophical Disenfranchisement of Art*. New York: Columbia University Press, 1986.

————. *Saul Steinberg: The Discovery of America*. New York: Alfred A. Knopf, 1992.

————. *The Transfiguration of the Commonplace: A Philosophy of Art*. Cambridge, Mass.: Harvard University Press, 1981.

Davidson, Donald. *Inquiries into Truth and Interpretation*. Oxford: Clarendon Press, 1984.

Davidson, S. *The Penguin Book of Political Comics*. Harmondsworth, Middlesex: Penguin, 1982.

Davis, Whitney. *Replications: Archaeology, Art History, Psychoanalysis*. University Park: The Pennsylvania State University Press, 1996.

Delany, Samuel R. "The Politics of Paraliterary Criticism." Typescript.

Denny, Don, and Judith O'Sullivan. *The Art of the Comic Strip*. Exhibition catalogue. College Park: University of Maryland, Department of Art, 1971.

Derrida, Jacques. *Of Grammatology*. Translated by Gayatri Chakravorty Spivak. Baltimore: Johns Hopkins University Press, 1976.

Dooley, Dennis, and Gary Engle. *Superman at Fifty! The Persistence of a Legend*. Cleveland: Oxtavia Press, 1987.

Dorfman, Ariel. *The Empire's Old Clothes: What the Lone Ranger, Babar, and Other Innocent Heroes Do to Our Minds*. New York: Pantheon, 1983.

Dorfman, Ariel, and Armand Mattelart. *How to Read Donald Duck: Imperialist Ideology in the Disney Comic*. Translated, with an introduction, by David Kunzle. New York: International General, 1975.

Dreyfus, Hubert L. *Being-in-the-World: A Commentary on Heidegger's "Being and Time," Division I*. Cambridge, Mass.: MIT Press, 1991.

Ecker, David W., and Stanley S. Madeka. *Pioneers in Perception: A Study of Aesthetic Perception*. St. Louis, Mo.: Cemrel, 1979.

Eco, Umberto. "The Myth of Superman." *Diacritics* 2, no. 1 (1972): 14–20.

————. "On 'Krazy Kat' and 'Peanuts.'" *New York Review* 32, no. 10 (1985): 25–27.

————. "The World of Charlie Brown." In *Apocalypse Postponed*, edited by Robert Lumley, chap. 2. Bloomington: Indiana University Press, 1994.

Eisner, Will. *Comics and Sequential Art*. Tamarac, Fla.: Poorhouse Press, 1985.

————. "Getting the Last Laugh: My Life in Comics." *New York Times Book Review*, 14 January 1990, 1, 26–27.

Elderfield, John. *Henri Matisse: A Retrospective*. Exhibition catalogue. New York: Museum of Modern Art, 1992.

Estren, Mark James. *A History of Underground Comics*. Berkeley: Ronin Publishing, 1987.

Fant, Ake. "The Case of the Artist Hilma af Klint." In *The Spiritual in Art: Abstract Painting, 1890–1985*, exhibition catalogue, by Maurice Tuchman, 154–63. Los Angeles: Los Angeles County Museum of Art, 1986.

Faus, Wolfgang Max, with R. Baird Shuman. "Comics and How to Read Them." *Journal of Popular Culture* 5 (summer 1971): 195–202.

Felstiner, Mary Lowenthal. *To Paint Her Life: Charlotte Salomon in the Nazi Era.* New York: HarperCollins, 1994.

Flam, Jack. *Matisse: The Man and His Art, 1869–1918.* Ithaca: Cornell University Press, 1986.

Flaubert, Gustave. *Sentimental Education.* Translated by Robert Baldick. London: Penguin, 1964.

Foucault, Michel. *Language, Counter-Memory, Practice: Selected Essays and Interviews.* Edited by Donald F. Bouchard. Ithaca: Cornell University Press, 1977.

Freedberg, S. J. *Painting in Italy, 1500 to 1600.* Harmondsworth, Middlesex: Penguin, 1971.

Fresnault-Druelle, Pierre. *La bande dessinée: L'univers et les techniques de quelques "comics" d'expression française.* Paris: Hachette, 1972.

Fried, Michael. *Absorption and Theatricality: Painting and Beholder in the Age of Diderot.* Berkeley and Los Angeles: University of California Press, 1980.

Froidevaux, Gérald. *Baudelaire: Représentation et modernité.* Paris: José Corti, 1989.

Fry, Roger. *Transformations: Critical and Speculative Essays on Art.* Garden City, N.Y.: Doubleday, 1956.

Fukuyama, Francis. *The End of History and the Last Man.* New York: Free Press, 1992.

Garber, Marjorie. *Dog Love.* New York: Simon & Schuster, 1996.

Genette, Gérard. *Narrative Discourse: An Essay in Method.* Translated by Jane E. Lewin. Ithaca: Cornell University Press, 1980.

———. *Narrative Discourse Revisited.* Translated by Jane E. Lewin. Ithaca: Cornell University Press, 1988.

Gifford, Denis. *Victorian Comics.* London: George Allen & Unwin, 1976.

Gimenez, Juan, and Roberto Dal Pra'. *Apocalypse: The Eyes of Doom.* Northampton, Mass.: Kitchen Sink Press, 1993.

Gombrich, E. H. *Art and Illusion.* Princeton: Princeton University Press, 1961.

———. *Meditations on a Hobby Horse.* London: Phaidon, 1963.

———. "Raphael's *Madonna Della Sedia.*" In *Norm and Form: Studies in the Art of the Renaissance,* 64–80. London: Phaidon, 1966.

Goodman, Nelson. *Languages of Art: An Approach to a Theory of Symbols.* Indianapolis: Hackett, 1976.

Gopnik, Adam. "Comics and Catastrophe." *New Republic,* 22 June 1987, 29–34.

———. "The Genius of George Herriman." *New York Review of Books* 33 (December 1986): 19–28.

Gorey, Edward. *The Glashycrumb Tinnies.* 1963. Reprinted in *Amphigorey.* New York: C. P. Putnam's Sons, 1972.

The Greatest Superman Stories Ever Told. New York: DC Comics, 1987.

Greenberg, Clement. *The Collected Essays and Criticism, Volume 4: Modernism with a Vengeance, 1957–1969.* Edited by John O'Brian. Chicago: University of Chicago Press, 1993.

Haas, Robert Bartlett. *Muybridge: Man in Motion.* Berkeley and Los Angeles: University of California Press, 1976.

Hannoosh, Michele. *Baudelaire and Caricature: From the Comic to an Art of Modernity.* University Park: The Pennsylvania State University Press, 1992.

Harris, Neil. "Who Owns Our Myths? Heroism and Copyright in an Age of Mass Culture." In *Cultural Excursions: Marketing Appetites and Cultural Tastes in Modern America,* chap. 11. Chicago: University of Chicago Press, 1990.

Harvey, Robert C. "The Aesthetics of the Comic Strip." *Journal of Popular Culture* 12 (1979): 640–52.

———. *The Art of the Funnies: An Aesthetic History.* Jackson: University Press of Mississippi, 1994.

Haskell, Francis, and Nicholas Penny. *Taste and the Antique: The Lure of Classical Sculpture, 1500–1900.* New Haven: Yale University Press, 1982.

Hegel, G. W. F. *Aesthetics: Lectures on Fine Art.* Translated by T. M. Knox. 2 vols. Oxford: Clarendon Press, 1975.

———. *The Phenomenology of Mind.* Translated by J. B. Baillie. New York: Harper & Row, 1967.

Heidegger, Martin. *Being and Time.* Translated by J. Macquarrie and E. Robinson. New York: Harper & Row, 1962.

Hergé. *The Adventures of Tintin: Reporter for "Le Petit Vingtième" in the Land of the Soviets.* 1929. Reprint, London: Sundancer, 1989.

———. *Les aventures de Tintin: Tintin au Congo.* Paris: Casterman, 1974.

———. *The Red Sea Sharks.* Boston: Little, Brown, 1970.

Herriman, George. *The Komplete Kat Komics.* Forestville, Calif.: Eclipse Books, 1988–91. (Vol. 1, 1916; vol. 3, 1918; vol. 5, 1920; vol. 6, 1921; vol. 7, 1922; vol. 8, 1923.)

———. *The Komplete Kolor Krazy Kat.* Vol. 1 (1935–36). Princeton, Wis.: Kitchen Sink Press, 1990.

———. *Krazy Kat.* Introduction by e. e. cummings. New York: Henry Holt, 1946.

———. *Krazy Kat Komix.* Vol. 5. Amsterdam: real free press, 1976.

Herwitz, Daniel. Review of *Poussin's Paintings,* by David Carrier. *Journal of Aesthetics and Art Criticism* 53, no. 3 (1995): 327.

Homer, William I., with John Talbot. "Eakins, Muybridge, and the Motion Picture Process." *Art Quarterly* 26, no. 2 (1963): 194–216.

hooks, bell. *Yearning: Race, Gender, and Cultural Politics.* Boston: South End Press, 1990.

Hughes, Robert. "The Rise of Andy Warhol." In *The First Anthology: Thirty Years of "The New York Review of Books,"* edited by R. Silvers, B. Epstein, and R. Hederman, 219–31. New York: New York Review of Books, 1993.

Inge, M. Thomas. *Comics as Culture.* Jackson: University Press of Mississippi, 1990.

Iser, Wolfgang. "The Reading Process: A Phenomenological Approach." In *Reader-Response Criticism: From Formalism to Post-Structuralism,* edited by Jane P. Tompkins, 49–71. Baltimore: Johns Hopkins University Press, 1980.

Jenkins, Patrick. *Flipbook Animation and Other Ways to Make Cartoons Move.* Toronto: Kids Can Press, 1991.

Kenney, Elise K., and John M. Merriman. *The Pear: French Graphic Arts in the Golden Age of Caricature.* Exhibition catalogue. South Hadley, Mass.: Mount Holyoke College Art Museum, 1991.

King, Tappan W. "The Image in Motion." *Journal of Popular Culture* 8 (1975): 11–18.

Kojève, Alexandre. *Introduction à la lecture de Hegel.* Paris: Gallimard, 1947.

Kris, Ernst, and E. H. Gombrich. "The Principles of Caricature." In *Psychoanalytic Explorations in Art,* by Ernst Kris, chap. 7. London: George Allen & Unwin, 1953.

Kunzle, David. *The Early Comic Strip: Narrative Strips and Picture Stories in the European Broadsheet from c. 1450 to 1825.* Berkeley and Los Angeles: University of California Press, 1973.

———. "Goethe and Caricature: From Hogarth to Töpffer." *Journal of the Warburg and Courtauld Institutes* 48 (1985): 164–88.

———. *The History of the Comic Strip: The Nineteenth Century.* Berkeley and Los Angeles: University of California Press, 1990.

Lacassin, Francis. "The Comic Strip and Film Language." *Film Quarterly* 25, no. 4 (1972): 11–23.

Larson, Gary. *The Chickens Are Restless.* Kansas City, Mo.: Andrews & McMeel, 1993.

———. *The Curse of Madame "C": A Far Side Collection.* Kansas City, Mo.: Andrews & McMeel, 1994.

———. *The Far Side Gallery.* Kansas City, Mo.: Andrews & McMeel, 1984.

———. *The Far Side Gallery 2.* Kansas City, Mo.: Andrews & McMeel, 1986.

———. *The Far Side Gallery 3.* Kansas City, Mo.: Andrews & McMeel, 1988.

———. *The Far Side Gallery 4.* Kansas City, Mo.: Andrews & McMeel, 1989.

———. *The Far Side Gallery 5.* Kansas City, Mo.: Andrews & McMeel, 1995.

———. *Last Chapter and Worse.* Kansas City, Mo.: Andrews & McMeel, 1997.

———. *The Prehistory of "The Far Side": A Tenth Anniversary Exhibit.* Kansas City, Mo.: Andrews & McMeel, 1989.

Laughton, Bruce. *Honoré Daumier.* New Haven: Yale University Press, 1996.

Lavin, Irving. "High and Low Before Their Time: Bernini and the Art of Social Satire." In *Modern Art and Popular Culture: Readings in High and Low,* edited by Kirk Varnedoe and Adam Gopnik, 8–51. New York: Abrams, 1990.

Lavin, Marilyn Aronberg. *The Place of Narrative: Mural Decoration in Italian Churches, 431–1600.* Chicago: University of Chicago Press, 1990.

Lee, Rensselaer W. *Ut Pictura Poesis: The Humanistic Theory of Painting.* New York: W. W. Norton, 1967.

Lessing, Gotthold Ephraim. *Laocoon: An Essay on the Limits of Painting and Poetry.* Translated by Ellen Frothingham. New York: Noonday Press, 1965.

Lichtenberg, Georg. *Lichtenberg's Commentaries on Hogarth's Engravings.* Translated by Innes Herdan and Gustav Herdan. London: Cresset Press, 1966.

Longhi, Roberto. *Caravaggio.* Rome: Editiori Riuniti, 1968.

Mackawa, Takeshi. *Victory for the Spirit.* Translated by Jonathan Clements. London: Bloomsbury Children's Books, 1995.

Mairowitz, David Zane, and Robert Crumb. *Introducing Kafka.* Northampton, Mass.: Kitchen Sink Press, 1994.

Marshall, Richard. *America's Great Comic-Strip Artists.* New York: Abbeville Press, 1989.

Marx, Karl, and Friedrich Engels. *Basic Writings on Politics and Philosophy.* Edited by Lewis S. Feuer. Garden City, N.Y.: Anchor Books, 1959.

McCay, Winsor. *The Complete Little Nemo in Slumberland.* Edited by Richard Marschall. Vols. 3–5. Ardsley, Pa.: Remco Worldservice Books, 1989–91.

McCloud, Scott. *Understanding Comics: The Invisible Art.* Northampton, Mass.: Kitchen Sink Press, 1993.

McDonnell, Patrick, Karen O'Connell, and Georgia Riley de Havenon. *Krazy Kat: The Comic Art of George Herriman.* New York: Abrams, 1986.

McLuhan, Marshall. *Understanding Media: The Extensions of Man.* New York: McGraw-Hill, 1964.

Medhurst, Andy. "Batman, Deviance, and Camp." In *The Many Lives of the Batman: Critical Approaches to a Superhero and His Media,* edited by Roberta E. Pearson and William Uricchio, 149–63. New York: Routledge, Chapman & Hall, 1991.

Meiss, Millard. *Painting in Florence and Siena After the Black Death: The Arts, Religion, and Society in the Mid-Fourteenth Century.* New York: Harper & Row, 1973.

Meiss, Millard, with Sharon Smith and Elizabeth Home Beatson. *French Painting in the Time of Jean de Berry: The Limbourgs and Their Contemporaries.* New York: George Braziller, 1974.

Miller, James. *The Passion of Michel Foucault.* New York: Anchor Books, 1993.

Morrison, Grant, Steve Yeowell, Jill Thompson, and Dennis Cramer. *The Invisibles: Say You Want a Revolution.* New York: DC Comics, 1996.

Nehamas, Alexander. "Mythology: The Theory of Plot." In *Essays in Aesthetics: Perspectives on the Work of Monroe C. Beardsley,* 180–96. Philadelphia: Temple University Press, 1983.

———. *Nietzsche: Life as Literature.* Cambridge, Mass.: Harvard University Press, 1985.

———. "Pity and Fear in *The Rhetoric* and *The Poetics.*" In *Aristotle's Rhetoric: Philosophical Essays,* edited by David J. Furley and Alexander Nehamas. Princeton: Princeton University Press, 1994.

———. "Plato and the Mass Media." *Monist* 71 (spring 1988): 214–34.

———. "The Postulated Author: Critical Monism as a Regulative Ideal." *Critical Inquiry* 8 (1981): 131–49.

———. "Serious Watching." In *The Interpretive Turn: Philosophy, Science, Culture,* edited by David R. Hiley, James F. Bohman, and Richard Shusterman, 260–81. Ithaca: Cornell University Press, 1991.

———. "What Did Socrates Teach and to Whom Did He Teach It?" *Review of Metaphysics* 46 (December 1992): 279–305.

———. "Writer, Text, Work, Author." In *Literature and the Question of Philosophy,* edited by Anthony J. Cascardi, 267–91. Baltimore: Johns Hopkins University Press, 1987.

Newcomb, Horace, ed. *Television: The Critical View.* 5th ed. New York: Oxford University Press, 1994.

Newhall, Beaumont. "Photography and the Development of Kinetic Visualization." *Journal of the Warburg and Courtauld Institutes* 7, nos. 1–2 (1944): 40–45.

O'Sullivan, Judith. *The Great American Comic Strip: One Hundred Years of Cartoon Art.* New York: Little, Brown, 1990.

Outcault, Richard Felton. *The Yellow Kid: A Centennial Celebration of the Kid Who Started Comics.* Southampton, Mass.: Kitchen Sink Press, 1995.

Pächt, Otto. *Book Illumination in the Middle Ages: An Introduction.* Translated by Kay Davenport. New York: Oxford University Press, 1984.

Panofsky, Erwin. *Meaning in the Visual Arts: Papers in and on Art History.* Garden City, N.Y.: Doubleday Anchor, 1955.

Peeters, Benoit. *Tintin and the World of Hergé.* Translated by Michael Farr. London: Methuen, 1989.

Plato. *The Republic of Plato.* Translated by Francis Macdonald Cornford. New York: Oxford University Press, 1945.

Podro, Michael. *The Critical Historians of Art*. New Haven: Yale University Press, 1982.

————. *The Manifold in Perception: Theories of Art from Kant to Hildebrand*. Oxford: Clarendon Press, 1972.

Psychoanalysis. West Plains, Mo.: Russ Cochran, 1988.

Quinn, Robert M. "Krazy's Dad: George Herriman, Creator of Krazy Kat." *Artspace: Southwestern Contemporary Arts Quarterly*, spring 1988, 29–46.

Rand, Archie (artist), and John Yau (writer). *Mug City Moves*. New York: A Monkey Choir, Maestros Production, 1991.

Reidelbach, Maria. *Completely Mad: A History of the Comic Book and Magazine*. Boston: Little, Brown, 1991.

Rey, Alain. *Les spectres de la bande: Essai sur la b.d.* Paris: Éditions de Minuit, 1978.

Richardson, John. *A Life of Picasso*. Vol. 1 (1881–1906). New York: Random House, 1991.

Roberts, Garyn G. *Dick Tracy and American Culture: Morality and Mythology, Text and Context*. Jefferson, N.C.: McFarland, 1993.

Rosemont. "Surrealism in the Comics I: Krazy Kat (George Herriman)." In *Popular Culture in America*, edited by Paul Buhle, 119–27. Minneapolis: University of Minnesota, 1987.

Rosenberg, Harold. *Saul Steinberg*. Exhibition catalogue. New York: Alfred A. Knopf, 1978.

Ross, Clifford, and Karen Wilkin. *The World of Edward Gorey*. New York: Abrams, 1996.

"Rube Goldberg." *Nemo* 24 (February 1987).

Sabin, Roger. *Adult Comics: An Introduction*. London: Routledge, 1993.

————. *Comics, Comix, and Graphic Novels*. London: Phaidon, 1996.

Salomon, Charlotte. *Charlotte: Life or Theater?* Translated by Leila Vennewitz. New York: Viking, 1981.

Schapiro, Meyer. "On Some Problems in the Semiotics of Visual Art: Field and Vehicle in Image Signs." *Semiotics* 1, no. 3 (1969): 223–42.

Scharf, Aaron. "Painting, Photography, and the Image of Movement." *Burlington Magazine* 10 (May 1962): 186–93.

Schiller, Friedrich. *On the Aesthetic Education of Man*. Translated by Elizabeth M. Wilkinson and L. A. Willoughby. Oxford: Clarendon Press, 1967.

Schmitt, Ronald. "Deconstructive Comics." *Journal of Popular Culture* 25 (1992): 153–61.

Schodt, Frederik L. *Manga! Manga! The World of Japanese Comics*. Tokyo: Kodansha International, 1983.

Scholes, Robert, and Robert Kellogg. *The Nature of Narrative*. London: Oxford University Press, 1966.

Schwartz, Gary. *Rembrandt: His Life, His Paintings*. New York: Viking, 1985.

Sedolsky, Lauren. Introduction to *Stephen Posen: New Paintings*, exhibition catalogue. New York: Jason McCoy, 1990.

Seldes, Gilbert. "The Krazy Kat That Walks by Himself." In *The Seven Lively Arts*, 207–19. New York: A. S. Barnes, 1957.

Shannon, Edward A. "'That We May Mis-unda-stend Each Udda': The Rhetoric of *Krazy Kat*." *Journal of Popular Culture*, 1983, 231–47.

Sheon, Aaron. "The Discovery of Graffiti." *Art Journal* 36, no. 1 (1975): 16–22.

Shiff, Richard. *Cézanne and the End of Impressionism*. Chicago: University of Chicago Press, 1984.

———. "Cézanne's Physicality: The Politics of Touch." In *The Language of Art History*, edited by S. Kemal and I. Gaskell, 53–77. Cambridge: Cambridge University Press, 1991.

Sparrow, John. *Visible Words: A Study of Inscriptions in and as Books and Works of Art*. Cambridge: Cambridge University Press, 1969.

Spiegelman, Art. *Maus*. New York: Pantheon, 1986.

———. *Maus II: A Survivor's Tale: And Here My Troubles Began*. New York: Pantheon, 1991.

Spiegelman, Art, and Françoise Mouly, eds. *Read Yourself Raw*. New York: Pantheon, 1987.

Steinberg, Leo. *Other Criteria: Confrontations with Twentieth-Century Art*. New York: Oxford University Press, 1972.

Stokes, Adrian. *The Critical Writings of Adrian Stokes*. 3 vols. London: Thames & Hudson, 1978.

Thomas, Frank, and Ollie Johnston. *Disney Animation: The Illusion of Life*. New York: Abbeville Press, 1981.

Vandromme, Pol. *Le monde de Tintin*. Paris: La Table Ronde, 1959.

Varnedoe, Kirk, and Adam Gopnik. *High and Low: Popular Culture and Modern Art*. New York: Museum of Modern Art, 1990.

Vasari, Giorgio. *The Lives of the Painters, Sculptors, and Architects*. Translated by A. B. Hinds. 4 vols. London: Everyman's Library, 1963.

Von Blum, Paul. "Comic-Strip Art." In *The Dictionary of Art*, edited by Jane Turner, 6:648–50. London: Macmillan, 1996.

Wallis, Mieczyslaw. "Inscriptions in Paintings." *Semiotica* 9 (1973): 1–28.

Warshaw, Robert. *The Immediate Experience: Movies, Comics, Theatre, and Other Aspects of Popular Culture*. Garden City, N.Y.: Doubleday, 1962.

Waught, Coulton. *The Comics*. New York: Macmillan, 1947.

Weber, Nicholas Fox. *The Art of Babar: The Work of Jean and Laurent de Brunhoff*. New York: Abrams, 1989.

Weitzmann, Kurt. *Illustrations in Roll and Codex: A Study of the Origin and Method of Text Illustration*. Princeton: Princeton University Press, 1947.

Wertham, Fredric. *Seduction of the Innocent*. New York: Rinehart, 1954.

West, Mark, et al. "Dr. Fredric Wertham." *Comics Journal* 123 (December 1989): 76–87.

White, Hayden. *The Content of the Form: Narrative Discourse and Historical Representation*. Baltimore: Johns Hopkins University Press, 1987.

Wiese, Ellen, ed. *Enter the Comics: Rodolphe Töpffer's Essay on Physiognomy and the True Story of Monsieur Crépin*. Lincoln: University of Nebraska Press, 1965.

Wilson, MaLin. "DemoKrazy in the American West." *Art Issues*, September/October 1997, 24–27.

Wittgenstein, Ludwig. *Philosophical Investigations*. Translated by G. E. M. Anscombe. New York: Macmillan, 1953.

Wölfflin, Heinrich. *Principles of Art History: The Problem of the Development of Style in Later Art*. Translated by M. D. Hottinger. New York: Dover, n.d.

Wollheim, Richard. *Art and Its Objects*. 2d ed. Cambridge: Cambridge University Press, 1980.

————. "Minimal Art." In *Art and the Mind*, 101–111. London: Allen Lane, 1973.

————. *Painting as an Art: The A. W. Mellon Lectures in the Fine Arts*. Princeton: Princeton University Press, 1987.

Wooley, Christ. *Wooley's History of the Comic Book*. Lake Buena Vista, Fla.: self-published, 1986.

Yee, Chiang. *Chinese Calligraphy: An Introduction to Its Aesthetic and Technique*. Cambridge, Mass.: Harvard University Press, 1973.

INDEX